What We Brought Across the River

Amber D. Inthavong

Copyright © 2025 Caribou Collective

All rights reserved.

ISBN: 979-8-218-75646-8

Introduction

As a little girl, I've wavered between embracing my identity as a Lao-American. Trying to find a balance between both cultures, I was unsure whether to wear it with pride or hide it. Although that has been my personal experience, it was more important to understand the experience of Mom and Dad first.

I was my parents' daughter, interpreter, their assistant, and their advocate. I had a responsibility to Mom and Dad from the very beginning, I was their voice in a world that did not speak our language. I carried the weight of ພາສາ (phasa), translating not only words but the spaces between them. I navigated the currents of a foreign land before I understood the depths myself. My small hands built a fragile bridge, spanning the gulf between their past and my present.

There are countless children like me—those who live with the echoes, the subtle expressions of love and sacrifice across silent generations. We carry stories of pain and resilience—tales of a homeland scarred by war yet blooming with hope.

I cannot tell the whole story that only my parents lived. They are stories etched into their skin and hearts, but I carry their shadows and light within me. This book is my ຄຳຂອງຄວາມຮັກ (kham khong khwam hak). This book is a tender tribute to their journey, to our family, and to a legacy that flows as deeply as the rivers of Laos, demanding to be remembered.

Contents

	Introduction	i
1	The Secret War	1
2	Mom and Dad	25
3	The Refugee Camp	38
4	America	Jan 23, 1980	70
5	Lao-American	99
6	Present Day	177
7	Return to the Motherland	190
8	The Aftermath	202
	Acknowledgements	209

1 | The Secret War

By the age of thirteen, I was already honing the skill of becoming invisible. Not in the way of magicians of course, I wasn't that type of kid. But I learned how to take up less space, and to blend into the beige-painted walls of my middle school. In the back row of history class, I sat silently, pressed into a molded blue plastic chair attached to a wooden desk that wobbled slightly when I shifted my weight.

I doubt kids use textbooks anymore these days, but back then, we were tasked with bringing them home to cover them with protective book covers. My textbook was wrapped in a brown paper bag from the grocery store I turned inside out and folded over like armor. I made small doodles drawn in pencil so lightly I could erase them if anyone leaned in too close.

The room buzzed around me with chairs scraping, chatter flying like paper airplanes, and someone tapping a pencil with the impatient rhythm of adolescence. I sat still, small, invisible with the goal to avoid drawing any attention.

Then there was Tory. She always claimed the seat right in front of mine, sliding into it with ease and smiling at me. She was everything I wasn't at thirteen. She was loud, unfiltered, and crackling with life. Her voice didn't just carry, it announced itself. She talked fast, laughed even faster, and seemed to have a radar for drama, especially when it involved the boys in our grade.

Her laugh would unfurl, curling into the corners of the classroom like smoke. Her green eyes were sharp, and she was a curious girl who never missed a thing. Especially not a thing about me.

She'd twist halfway around in her seat before the bell rang, her long hair brushing across my wooden desk. I'd half expect her to make fun of me about something but she never did. She'd ask things like, "Do you think Josh is cute?" or, "Oh my god, did you see Mr. H's shirt today?" I'd mutter whatever came to mind, worried I'd reply with the wrong thing, "Yeah, I guess," or "It's…definitely a choice."

That's when she'd laugh—not mockingly, but like she'd just discovered a big secret about me. She'd lean in close, elbows on my desk, so close I could see the tiny constellation of freckles across her nose. "You're funny!" she'd say, as if she knew me so well. I never knew what to do with that, but I'd nod and accept what she gave me.

There was something about the way Tory kept pulling me into her orbit. Like she was trying to tug me out of my shell just by showing up, day after day. She didn't ask for anything in return, not a secret, not a laugh, not even a smile. Just my presence. And in middle school, it was kind of nice not to have anything expected of me.

Maybe she thought I was a mystery. Maybe I was just a space for her voice to go. Or maybe she was kind, in the rare way some people are before the world teaches them to stop being that way. Either way, I didn't mind.

It was rare to come across kids like her in my school.

Middle school is a strange kind of terrain. Everyone's pretending not to be terrified, stumbling through their own private storms while trying to look cool doing it. Everyone was already growing concerned about levels of popularity and which crowds they were associated with.

Girls were already pairing off with boys like it was a game of musical chairs no one wanted to lose. And while I always noticed the boys, I knew better than to even try. The very act of talking to a boy wouldn't be a good outcome for me, and would only result in humiliating myself. I barely understood the unfamiliar curves of my own body, let alone how I was supposed to act like I belonged inside it.

We didn't come prepared for puberty. It slipped in like a fog—unwanted and unexpected when we weren't ready for it. My insecurities felt bigger than anyone else's, though I now suspect everyone was walking around with some kind of doubt inside of them that maybe they didn't know how to name. So I stayed quiet. I shrank. I obeyed because it was what my parents taught me to do.

I never forgot Tory, someone who was so bold, brilliant, and utterly uninterested in hiding. We weren't friends, not really. But in every class we shared, she was a steady presence in my day. Like a flare in the fog, reminding me I wasn't completely lost.

She was part of that strange constellation of kids I couldn't quite come into. They were the band kids and the color guard crew, who spun flags at school sporting events like they were extensions of their souls. Her world was loud and layered with inside jokes and secrets. My world was noisy too, but with anxious thoughts, masked so no one would know it.

Even now, when I think back to those years, it's not the classes, the lockers, or awkward school dances that stood out as much to me as she did. The people like her. The people I wanted to be more like. All while I was too focused on being a girl who spent most of her childhood trying not to call too much attention.

I didn't realize it then, but something about those brief interactions between us began to leave a mark. They sat and lived in the corners of me, where my thoughts and feelings lived. A place where I never let anyone into as a kid. Especially not my parents.

At home, I tried to be the 'good daughter.' Who cleared her plate, finished her homework, and kept her feelings folded beneath her *Babysitters Club* and *Goosebumps* books from the school library.

My parents had enough to worry about after all, the bills, long shifts, and improving their broken English. They were tired most days, moving through life like it was something they had to survive, rather than enjoy. I'm sure my silence was much appreciated when it fit neatly into the margins of their exhaustion. It was easier that way.

Then came the history assignment: a presentation on any country of our choice. I chose Denmark. It was small, neutral, and safely unfamiliar. I didn't know much about it, but that was part of the draw—it was clean and crisp in the textbook, with plenty of facts and cheerful pictures of windmills, pastries, and bikes. The kind of country no one would question me about really. No one would squint at me when I said its name.

At home, my older sister Saeng helped me pull it all together. Being ten years older, she had the practical wisdom of someone who'd been through all this before and had little patience for frilly displays. She knew exactly how to slap a project together and make it look like effort. While I cut out pictures of Danish open-faced sandwiches and colorful row houses, she glued the edges, pressed them down flat.

"Where's Laos?" I said under my breath, flipping through the thick, glossy textbook on the living room floor.

Saeng didn't even look up. "You're not gonna find it," she said, brushing a corner of glue off her fingertips. "Believe me."

The certainty in her voice stopped me. Maybe she had looked for it before. Maybe she'd felt the same ache of being invisible, spent time scanning the pages, hoping our homeland would be there, printed in ink, proof that it mattered.

But there was nothing there. So I went on with Denmark. Wrote my facts in all caps on color-coded flashcards. Practiced in front of the bathroom mirror, standing straight, speaking loud. When I gave my presentation, no one asked questions about it. I got an A. I had made the safe choice.

But deep down, I knew the truth: I had chosen a country that came with built-in permission. Denmark was in the book. It belonged in the classroom. Laos didn't.

It nagged at me. That strange absence—how a whole country could be missing, erased without apology. It clung to me long after the poster board went into the recycling bin. I started wondering why no one ever talked about Laos. Why the place my parents came from had vanished between the chapters of European wars and American triumphs. Why my teacher never mentioned it and more importantly why the hell I never asked.

That year, we studied resilience and human rights. We learned about the Holocaust, the Underground Railroad, internment camps, and revolutions. Students raised their hands, offering up family stories like treasured heirlooms. They spoke of great-grandparents who fled persecution, fought for civil rights, and shared names that were etched in history.

I sat wondering if my people had stories like that too. Had we ever been brave? What did my parents live through before I existed? What had they run from? But I didn't ask then. I didn't yet know how to hold those questions, let alone speak them aloud. What I did know at the time was, my parents had escaped something and they never wanted to look back. They spoke of Laos carefully. Their memories were like glass that was fragile and sharp at the edges.

Instead, they focused on the present. On making it

here. On keeping the lights on, the refrigerator full. The unspoken message was clear, be grateful. You're lucky to be here. Don't look behind you.

And I listened. For a long time, I did. But as the years passed, I started searching on my own. I spent late nights on the internet once we had access to it, finding foreign articles, and names of bombings I'd never heard of in school.

What I uncovered was staggering: the Secret War. A campaign so violent and sustained it scattered generations like seeds. Over two million tons of explosives and villages flattened. Families forced to flee through jungles, across rivers, and into refugee camps.

No one had taught us this. No one had told me that the missing stories in my history books wasn't an oversight—it was erasure. And yet, for as little as I was, it was mine to figure out.

For those of you who, like me, never found Laos in your school books, let me introduce you to this small but beautiful country nestled into the heart of Southeast Asia.

Of course, I'm biased. But Laos is one of the most extraordinary places I've ever traveled to thus far. There's something about the way the sun hangs low over the mountains, the way the air carries the smell of lemongrass and smoke from open cooking fires, the way people wave to strangers like they've known them forever. The villages have a special magic that pulses gently beneath the surface.

The people are kind. The land is generous. The trees

are tall, wide and hum stories when the wind blows just right. Rice fields stretch endlessly, soaking up light like mirrors. And then there are the elephants that are so sacred to the Lao people that our country's old flag once bore three of them, standing side by side on a pedestal beneath a parasol. In Lao culture, elephants symbolize luck, peace, and prosperity. For centuries, they were more than animals. They were our guardians.

Despite its small size, Laos has a big history that is layered with both richness and sorrow. Landlocked, bordered by Thailand to the west and Vietnam to the east, it often sits in the shadows of its neighbors. The Mekong River marks its western edge—a deep, winding current that separates Laos from Thailand, though the cultures flow into one another like water.

Laos is not one single voice. It is a chorus of over 160 ethnic groups, each with their own dialects, traditions, and beliefs. In some cases, two Lao people from different regions might not even understand each other's words. But still, they'll smile. Still, they'll offer food. Still, they'll find a way to connect. That's just how it is and who we are.

Food is more than a way to spark up special memories in Laos, it's also our love language. And if you were raised in a Lao home, you know that sticky rice isn't just food, but it's an extension of your hand. It is shaped into small, warm clumps, perfect for scooping sauces or pinching bites of grilled meat. It's comfort. It's culture. I grew up on sticky rice and still crave it when I feel far from myself.

Lao mothers, including mine, expect a lot. They speak loudly, not out of anger, but with the force of generations. As my mother always says, "If I don't say it like I mean it, how will you listen?" Children are expected to listen, help, and contribute. In many villages, they wake before the sun, fetch water, sweep the yards, help with the market or farm. Respect isn't requested, it's instilled in us early.

Marriage, too, carries immense meaning. It's not just a personal event, but it's communal. Weddings spill into the streets, along with drums and laughter that will repeat for hours. A whole village might turn out to celebrate. Lao people find a reason to drink for anything—the birth of a new baby, weddings, funerals, good harvests, or bad news. Drinking isn't just about the alcohol. It's a kind of liquid language that's more about ritual and togetherness.

And then there's the heart of it all: Buddhism. Theravada Buddhism flows through daily life like a second river. Temples rise from the hills like golden beacons, and the morning air is often filled with the soft, melodic chanting of monks, endless and soothing. You don't have to be religious to feel it. Walk into any *wat* (temple), and you can feel everything shift around you. There's incense in the air, gold covered statues, a stillness that makes you forget the world outside. The Buddha gazes down from towering altars, serene and with life wisdom.

Even as a child, walking barefoot on the cool marble floor into a temple, an immense energy would overcome me. It was slow and profound, like being seen by something ancient.

At one point in history, the French declared Laos part of French Indochina, drawn by its strategic location and the promise of the Mekong River. That crucial river that is wide, winding, and alive with trade—was the lifeblood of Southeast Asia, and the French knew it. They wanted control, and for a time, they got it.

The French presence left its fingerprints on the country in ways that still linger to this day. In the crisp crust of a banh mi, a baguette tucked into a sandwich layered with pickled vegetables and sliced meats. The French are also present in the curved balconies and pale stucco facades of colonial buildings that still exist now. In Vientiane (Vang-Chun), Laos' capital, stands the Patuxai—our own towering war monument. Modeled after Paris' Arc de Triomphe, it rises not to celebrate conquest, but to honor those who fought for freedom. A monument born from occupation, now a symbol of resilience.

But our independence from France came at a cost. Laos slipped from one foreign influence into another. Once French control began to crumble across Southeast Asia, the vacuum was filled by new powers—chief among them, Ho Chi Minh, the revolutionary communist leader from neighboring Vietnam.

Having driven out the French from his own country, he turned his focus to Laos and the strategic Mekong River once more.

WHAT WE BROUGHT ACROSS THE RIVER

With Ho Chi Minh's influence, a radical communist movement took root: the Pathet Lao. Backed by Vietnamese support, the Pathet Lao quickly gained traction, aligning themselves with North Vietnam and the Soviet Union. It was the perfect storm, and Laos—small, landlocked, and poorly understood—was caught in the middle.

Fearing the spread of communism across Southeast Asia, the United States stepped in. Under President Dwight D. Eisenhower, the infamous Domino Theory took shape. He believed strongly that if Laos fell to communism, so would all of Southeast Asia including Cambodia, Thailand, Malaysia and Indonesia.

Before he prepared to leave office, Eisenhower discreetly authorized a covert operation—a secret mission to train the CIA and anti-communist forces inside Laos to combat communism. Their objective: disrupt the Ho Chi Minh Trail, which was a vital supply route that snaked through east Laos and fed the war machine in Vietnam with their essentials.

And so began what history would call the Secret War. When President John F. Kennedy stepped into office, Eisenhower briefed him directly on the mission. He passed the torch and responsibility over to Kennedy. As part of the plan, Kennedy, young and idealistic, first publicly pledged support for Laos' neutrality. In 1962, the International Agreement on the Neutrality of Laos was signed. It was an agreement that forbade any foreign military involvement. But it was largely a mirage and a ploy in their plan, to get everyone to let their guard down. Because once neutrality was signed and in place, behind closed doors, he was following through with Eisenhower's Secret War as promised.

With the world's attention elsewhere, the United States moved unnoticed. The CIA began working to establish a local army in Laos—a force that could move through the dense jungle, knew the terrain, and had something personal at stake.

They found their answer in a man named Vang Pao. A general in the Royal Lao Army who was a fierce leader among the Hmong (Mong) people, Vang Pao had already fought the Japanese in World War II and battled Viet Minh during the First Indochina War. He had the perfect credentials. His past had prepared him for a battle just like this. He had lost villages, comrades, maybe even parts of himself before, but most importantly he was angry and ready to fight back. That history carved a deep resistance within him—especially toward Vietnamese communists. The CIA saw all of it: his loyalty, his experience, and his leadership. But what made him invaluable was the deep bond he had with the Hmong people.

The Hmong tribe of Laos had always lived differently. High in the mountains, in remote northern villages, they farmed with the rhythm of the seasons. Unlike the majority of Laos, who were Buddhist, they believed in spirits. The Hmong followed very different religious and ancestral beliefs. Their world was filled with signs and meanings invisible to most outsiders. Shamans guided the sick and dying through realms unseen, and intricate embroidery—*paj ntaub* (pahn-dow)—told the stories of clans, of love, of loss.

Where a majority of the Lao population practiced Theravada Buddhism, the Hmong followed animist traditions. My mom would call it old world beliefs. It was one of the most profound cultural rifts between the Lao majority and the Hmong tribe—evidence that even being part of the same country, identity could fracture in complicated ways.

Historically marginalized, the Hmong were often viewed as outsiders in their own homeland. That isolation, combined with a long-standing distrust of centralized power, made them more willing to ally with the Americans. When Vang Pao was asked to join in the fight against communism, he and the Hmong people did so willingly and without fear. Not just for ideology—but for the goal of something better. A Laos where their children might grow up safe. Seen. Free.

The CIA saw in them a perfect partner. Vang Pao and the Hmong people had knowledge of the land that was unmatched. Their loyalty, unwavering. They guided American pilots through narrow mountain passes, built secret airstrips, and launched daring raids against communist strongholds to disrupt the Ho Chi Minh trail supply route to Vietnam. They became the eyes, ears, and heartbeat of the CIA's Secret Army.

They paid dearly for it. Air America, a CIA-controlled airline, became their lifeline—delivering supplies, weapons, and medicine. Planes landed in narrow valleys barely wide enough to hold them, their engines kicking up red dust. The mission, which began with a modest budget of five million in the early 1960s, ballooned. By 1962, costs had more than doubled. By the end of the decade, the U.S. was spending nearly half a billion dollars each year—money flowing into a war it refused to publicly admit existed.

But money couldn't shield what was coming. The Hmong had committed everything, their homes, lives, and lineage, to a cause that existed in the shadows. And for all the promises made in hushed meetings and coded transmissions, the cost of that allegiance would stretch far beyond the battlefield.

Today, Mom sat stoically across from me in her bedroom to recall the past. She perched on a wooden chair with a worn cushion, its fabric threadbare from years of use. Her posture was steady, but her eyes flickered, as if her memories were too heavy to hold all at once. For a moment, she looked away. The war was still there—buried but not forgotten, living in the soft shadows behind her gaze.

Her memories began in her childhood home in Luang Namtha (Long-Numb-Ta), northern Laos. At nearly sixty-six years old, she seemed smaller now, more delicate than before. But she had always been this small, just five feet tall, and it was I who had grown big enough to notice. Her skin, still smooth with barely a wrinkle, she credited to her daily use of sunscreen. She looked fragile, but I knew better. Her softness was only on the surface. Inside, she was forged from something much harder.

WHAT WE BROUGHT ACROSS THE RIVER

I sat on a chair in front of her with a pencil in hand, ready to listen, ready to scribble whatever pieces of history she could offer. But instead of solemnity, there was a soft grin on her face. Her head was wrapped in a plastic bag, waiting for the timer to beep so she could rinse the box dye from her hair. That detail struck me—this woman who had carried the weight of war in her chest was dyeing her hair and making small talk with me, unsure where to begin.

Eventually, she did. She started with a memory from when she was eight years old. Back then, the war hadn't reached their village yet, but it had begun. And they had no way of knowing that the war was going to last for nearly ten years long.

Life was simple, slow, and intimate in Luang Namtha. The villagers lived off the land and the river, which served every purpose imaginable, from bathing, to laundry, and even dishes. My mom laughed gently as she spoke of running barefoot with her brothers and sisters, their tiny bodies balancing heavy water buckets strung on bamboo poles.

Their home, like most others, stood on wooden stilts with dirt for a yard. The air was thick with the scent of steaming rice, the sound of chickens clucking and children calling out to one another. It was a drastic contrast to the childhood I had.

In that simplicity, the harshness of the world felt far away. Until the morning it all changed. Her father—my grandfather, Kongkeo—left the house to bring food to her Uncle Teng, who was a known anti-communist fighter. While Uncle Teng was not a Hmong soldier, he was in fact one of the rare Lao men who was unafraid to oppose the Pathet Lao. So he joined. This made him dangerous to know, as even associating with Uncle Teng could put the entire family at risk.

The people in the village held their breath every time Kongkeo made the journey, but he insisted on bringing his brother a hot meal. He had been leaving every morning for weeks to bring him food despite the risk. But on this particular morning, as he said goodbye to his wife and children, it would be the last time he would ever see them again.

One day passed. Then two. Then ten. My grandmother stood in the doorway each evening, her eyes combing the horizon for a silhouette that never appeared. Her faith faded a little more with each sunset she met.

And then a man came—an ex-prisoner, frantic and breathless—carrying the kind of truth that fractures families. The unknown man had escaped a communist prison, and there, in makeshift cells that were dug into the muddy ground, with bars that close overhead, he had witnessed Kongkeo being captured too. Alive, but barely. He was caught bringing Uncle Teng food and had been accused of being an American informant, beaten, starved, and tortured for answers he did not have.

The man's voice shook as he described what he saw, and my grandmother, wild-eyed, peppered him with questions. She even asked if he had seen Uncle Teng, but he had no news to bring about his whereabouts. He only had one image in his mind to share: Kongkeo, a man who had nothing to do with the cause, who was now out there captured and barely holding on.

There was no one to call for help. No government to appeal to. The truth was, reaching out to authorities would only result in the communists themselves showing up on your doorstep. They quickly realized that no help was available to them, paralyzing them and leaving them helpless.

My mom was too young to understand the full gravity of what happened. She only knew that her father was gone. That the house felt heavier. That her mother's sobs came with a sorrow that muffled through the dark in the middle of the night thereafter. She tried to sleep, but the emptiness was deafening. She prayed, hands clasped tightly, for her father to walk back through their doorway like nothing had changed. But he never did.

My grandmother, knowing danger was closing in, made a choice: she would not wait to become a target. If Pathet Lao soldiers believed Kongkeo was an informant, they might come for her and her children next. She imagined them beating him to oblivion until he named where his home was and where he came from that morning. And so, she made a decision she thought she would never have to make. She gathered all nine of her children—nine—and fled.

It was survival. It was strength. But to my mom, it felt like a loss all over again. Leaving their home meant leaving behind the last place her father had been. What if he returned? What if he found nothing but an empty house and a cold hearth?

Still, they left. They fled as far west as possible to Houayxay (Hoy-Sai), over 100 miles west of their own village. A place pressed along the Laos-Thailand border. It was seemingly the perfect place to disappear. But even there, the war's breath was not far. The U.S. was bombing relentlessly in the years that followed—over 580,000 missions riddled east of where they were, more than all the bombs dropped in World War II combined. The explosions may have been far from Houayxay, but the fear was not. It lingered in every conversation, behind every glance. It was woven into the fabric of their lives.

Most of my mom's memories growing up were during that long war. The war was a continuous backdrop of her adolescence, like a storm she had learned to live with in the background. Turmoil she would have to learn to become desensitized to.

In their new village of Houayxay, she carried on even with all the unknowns in her heart. She walked to school with her friends, fetched water, swept floors, and helped raise her younger siblings. Her mother worked endlessly to keep them fed and upright. The villagers murmured constantly about the communists, about the Americans, but no one really knew who to believe. Trust became dangerous. Silence became instinct.

As each year unfolded, the war seemingly felt like it would never end. Mom spent many nights praying the communists would lose, believing the U.S. had enough firepower and strength to make them fold so this would all be over. They waited for its conclusion—for peace, for news, for something to change. But most of all, they waited, wondering whether they would survive the war they never asked for.

And yet, through it all, my mother tried to hold onto what little was left of her childhood. The memories of her father. The village they'd abandoned. The version of herself that hadn't yet been hollowed out by war. She held it like a fragile object she couldn't let herself lose. She was a little girl too young to mourn, but too wise to forget.

When she finished speaking, the timer beeped. The bag came off her head, and she walked to the bathroom to rinse out the dye, as if she hadn't just opened a door to a painful part of herself. I sat frozen, my pencil still in hand, the page in front of me now crowded with notes and cross-outs and margins full of questions. But the truth was, there was nothing left to write. I wasn't thinking about facts anymore. I was feeling something deeper for my mom.

For most of my life, I had kept my Lao identity like a secret about myself—present, but not spoken. I spoke English better than Lao. I wore jeans and listened to pop and r&b music. I grew up in a country where no one knew how to pronounce my last name, let alone find my country on a map. I thought that meant it wasn't worth mentioning. That ignoring it was easier.

After listening to my mother's story, I was moved. I had always known, in the vaguest terms, that my parents escaped the war. That phrase was repeated like punctuation when people asked about our past. But now, escaping meant something more. It meant a barefoot girl fleeing a village under threat, it meant heartache and displacement, and it meant losing a father to a system that punished resistance with death. And now despite decades in a new land with a new family, the grief she had carried for so long still came back, soft yet persistent, like a memory that wouldn't fade.

All this time, she'd been carrying on with her life, never knowing what really happened to her father. Like a parent who had a missing child and their photo printed on milk cartons. She would never know what happened. The more I sat with Mom's story, the more I understood that what I thought was distance from my heritage had actually been absent for a reason.

No teacher had ever told me about my country's past. No textbook had mentioned Laos. And even in college, when students spoke of ancestry and roots, I felt like mine were buried too deep to name out loud. And because I never learned, I didn't have anything to offer. It was all supposed to be a secret.

This invisibility wasn't an accident, it was a consequence. A consequence of war, of politics, of migration, of survival. My parents sacrificed their voices so we could all have safety. They had shed some of themselves to give us armor in a safe place. I was fluent in assimilation, and I thought that fluency made me strong. Now I wasn't so sure.

After that day in my mother's room, I began to look

inward more often. I started asking questions I once avoided: What else had I missed? What else had my family protected me from behind their occasional half grins and a busy kitchen? I returned to stories I had brushed aside, family photos I hadn't studied closely, memories I had thought were ordinary but were actually soaked in survival.

The more I learned, the more I felt the lines between then and now blur. My mother's story wasn't just hers. It was the beginning of my sister's, my brother's, and mine. Not because we had lived through the same losses, but because we had been shaped by Mom and Dad's echoes. Her displacement was the start of what made room for our wonderful lives. Her fear had made space for our freedom.

And now that I knew, I couldn't unknow. The past wasn't a foreign country. It was home. I was just learning how to return to it.

As the last days of the war wore on, the resistance weakened. The jungle hills once reverberating with the sounds of allied determination, were now settling into exhaustion and grief. The bombers stopped flying. The planes that once dropped food and medicine began to vanish from the sky. Vang Pao's Hmong soldiers—tired, starved, ravaged by disease—began to fall in a slow, agonizing unraveling. The dream of a free Laos began to fade, slipping further with each breathless day. They were unsuccessful against the communists and unable to stop the supply route of supplies going into Vietnam.

The Pathet Lao, more powerful and more ruthless

than ever, ultimately emerged victorious. The communists won and the U.S. CIA crumbled in their operation. Their triumph marked the final collapse of the anti-communist forces, a devastating end to a war that had already taken too much.

In desperation of their loss to the communists, the CIA and the White House made one final move. Vang Pao and his family were evacuated by helicopter to Thailand. A few planes followed—small, overloaded, fueled by sheer panic and last chances. Only around 2,500 Hmong made it out that way. The rest were left to fend for themselves, scrambling for a seat on departing planes, shoving, clawing, pushing others off the ledge in a frantic bid to survive.

For the thousands that were left behind, escape meant a brutal journey by foot—crossing jungle, rivers, and mountain paths under the constant threat of death to try and get to the safe haven of Thailand. The Pathet Lao communists hunted them like animals. There was no amnesty, no second chance.

Just days after Vang Pao's evacuation, thousands of Hmong civilians were slaughtered on the Hin Heup Bridge as they tried to flee. Those who surrendered were still executed. They were traitors to the Pathet Lao communist. Even the Hmong people who didn't participate in the fight, were still marked as traitors. There was no mercy. No escape. No future.

My mother and her family had fled their home village in the earliest stages of the war, far before it reached its most violent finale. But as the country eventually collapsed in 1975, even their earliest escape felt like foreshadowing. A precaution that became prophecy.

What began as a quiet migration to avoid conflict, now turned into a desperate exodus for an entire nation. The U.S. and its Hmong allies, once dominant players, fled the region in fear. The Lao people followed in droves, terrified of what the new regime might bring.

The end of the Secret War didn't bring peace. It brought more devastation. It stole one in every ten Laotians. It even cost hundreds of American lives, who were part of the U.S. CIA. Once the dust finally settled, a quarter of Laos's population—families like mine—were left scattering, displaced and broken, with nothing to return to. The rest fled further west toward Thailand, heading as far away from the Vietnam border as possible. The people were driven by terror, hunger, and the slim chance that safety might wait on the other side.

Under the rule of the Pathet Lao, Laos was no longer a homeland. It was a trap. Since every Hmong man, woman, and child was branded a traitor, their only choice was to leave or die. For the rest of the general Lao population, if they posed any threat to the new rule, they were sent to brutal reeducation camps. They worked until their bodies gave out, starved into submission, silenced into obedience. Prisons overflowed with the brightest minds—doctors, teachers, poets, and politicians—stripped of their voices and thrown into darkness. The very people who could rebuild the country were the biggest threat of all to the Pathet Lao.

The new regime wasted no time rewriting the narrative. Journalists were imprisoned. Dissenters disappeared. Laos sealed itself off from the world, and inside its borders, everything fell like ash. The stories of what happened were buried—erased before they could ever be told.

The Pathet Lao called it equality. They called it a revolution. But it was repression, plain and raw. The Marxist-Leninist ideology demanded uniformity—no one richer, no one smarter, no one allowed to dream outside the walls of the state. A country once vibrant with culture and history was painted over in dull grays. The dream they promised was a nightmare for those who had to live it.

And so, Laos became a land of ghosts. Memories dissolved into secrets. Loved ones had gone missing if not dead amongst the chaos of scattering from bullets and bombs. Grief became part of their routine. And the proud people who once called this place home learned to live under the weight of something they could not name but could never escape.

The war was over. But the pain was only just beginning.

2 | Mom & Dad

Mom and Dad were married the same year Pathet Lao claimed victory. Laos was officially a communist ruled country. After all the death and destruction, the nation was left in an eerie, unsettling quiet, haunted by the remnants of what had been. For those who were still alive, who had not run or been thrown into a reeducation camp yet, they were sitting and waiting for what was to come next. The new government was sweeping through Laos slow and steady like a dark tide. But in the small west village of Houayxay, a different story was just beginning.

Both of them were still teenagers when they met, standing at the fragile threshold between youth and survival, during the final, unrelenting days of the war. History was unfolding behind the scenes in the fire and ash of the east, but their decisions—so personal and full of promise—would shape the course of my life.

It began on a bright spring afternoon. Mom was walking home from school with three of her classmates, their steps familiar along the village path they took each day. The sun hung dimly in the smoky sky, as though the wind had swept over the traces of the war, while the sound in the streets filled with the quiet rhythm of vendors closing up shop.

Along the way, they passed a small food stand—a makeshift structure of bamboo poles and table sheets, fragrant with the smell of herbs and fermented spice.

Behind the stall stood a cheerful woman, her face open with laughter, selling bowls of *khao lafoon* (cow la-foon), a northern Lao favorite made with chilled tomato broth, fermented bean paste, and slippery tapioca squares.

As the girls approached, the woman called out with a wink, "I have one last bowl left, whoever eats it can become my new daughter-in-law!"

They all laughed at the absurdity of it, but to everyone's surprise, Mom stepped forward to show off, pulled out a few Lao kip from her pocket, and bought the last bowl. Her friends erupted into teasing. "Well, now you have to marry her son!" they jeered. Mom played along, slurping the last bite with a smirk and then, half-curious, asked, "So, where is your son, anyway?"

The woman gestured toward a temple across the road. "He's a monk there," she said proudly. It was a temple the girls passed every day, its orange-robed novices sweeping the courtyard or carrying alms bowls at dawn. At the time, it all felt like a harmless joke—until Mom would soon learn that the woman at the food stand would, in fact, become her mother-in-law after all.

In 1974, Dad made a decision that would change everything. He left the temple. Like many Lao boys, he had entered as a novice monk when he was still small, his head shaved, his days filled with scripture, chants, and the structured serenity of Theravada Buddhism. It was a path taken not out of ambition but obligation, a spiritual rite that brought honor to the family. But the world outside the temple was unraveling fast. As communist rule was now their inevitable fate, they all knew monks were no longer protected. Intellectuals, teachers, and religious figures would continue to be viewed as threats to the new government—symbols of the old world, of independent thought and moral authority. The safety Dad once knew behind temple walls began to dissolve.

He was ready to come down from the temple steps and rejoin the world as a boy again. The country was teetering, and no one had the luxury of adolescence anymore. But even in the uncertainty of those years, Mom and Dad found something that looked a lot like a beginning.

Their first meeting was sweetly orchestrated through friends, one of those lighthearted teenage match-ups that felt more like a joke than a real possibility. Mom's friend was dating one of Dad's friends, and together they decided to play matchmaker. A double date was their mission—simple, wishful, awkward in the way only teenage plans can be.

What followed was a comedy of innocence. Neither Mom nor Dad knew how to write a proper love letter. They were fourteen, unsure of what real love even meant, but their friends were eager to play go-betweens. In an act of pure mischief, the first notes exchanged between them weren't written by either of them at all.

Dad's friend wrote the first letter, pretending to be Dad, and gave it to Mom. In turn, Mom's friend replied on behalf of Mom, with even more sweetness and flair than she would have dared on her own. Mom and Dad had no idea, but back and forth they went—reading letters filled with borrowed words, clumsy compliments, and promises neither of them had written, yet both secretly enjoyed.

It was a beginning straight out of a romantic comedy. But it was also their rebellion against the world around them, a world falling apart with fear and displacement, where something so innocent could still bloom. Love, in their case, began not with authenticity, but with imagination. With make-believe in a world where turmoil didn't exist. Perhaps that's what made it real, not so much the words themselves, but the little thrill of being noticed, chosen, and seen.

I never grew up seeing my parents hold hands. They rarely embraced in front of us, never kissed on the cheek. As a child, I don't think I noticed at first—it was just how they were. Their love existed, subdued, practiced, and sealed behind closed doors. To me and my siblings, they were simply Mom and Dad: dependable, unflinching, always working, always watching. I guess over time their bond became forged more in duty than affection, in survival rather than sentiment.

But what once looked like emotional distance, could be seen as resilience. With everything I've come to learn about their past, maybe there's more to it. A kind of love that isn't showy or verbal, but tucked into the small acts: the way Dad wouldn't go to a party if Mom didn't want to go too, or the way they insisted you always eat more—even if you were already full.

Their love was born in a country that was collapsing. They met when the world around them was burning down, when each day carried a new uncertainty. There was no space for softness, no room for romantic declarations. Affection, in that kind of world, had to look like protection. Feelings had to be hidden, because expressing your feelings about anything could get you killed.

My Dad, who once left the temple to become a teenage husband, would never talk about love as something poetic or sweet. But he built a life for us with hands that had once carried Buddhist prayer. He was always fixing things—home projects, fences, cars—and I think that's how he showed his love: by repairing the world around us so we would never have to feel how broken it was the way he had to. My mother, on the other hand, kept our lives in rhythm. She cooked, cleaned, juggled jobs and kids, and never once asked for thanks. Her love was logistical, invisible—seen only when it was missing.

I wondered how they held onto each other all these years. There were arguments, moments of tension thick with unspoken history, and days they moved around one another like shadows sharing the same space. But then I'd catch the small things, the way Dad always made sure Mom's gas tank was full before her errands, or how Mom kept Dad's favorite dishes warm even when he came home late. There was something there, in the way they always looked out for each other.

Their love was shaped by war. Not just the one they lived through, but the one that never left them. The kind of war that hides in the body, long after the fighting stops. It shaped how they raised us, how they protected each other, how they navigated a country that never asked who they were or what they had lost. They didn't need to say I love you out loud. Their whole lives were proof of it.

And maybe, as children of survivors, we learn to read between the lines. To hear love in what isn't said after a long day. In the sound of sticky rice being flipped in the wicker basket. In a glance across the room when no one else is looking. Their love may not have looked like the movies. But it held. Through war, through escape, through resettlement. It held.

Their wedding was modest, stitched together with what little they had. A colorful *sinh* (sin) tied at Mom's waist, borrowed jewelry from cousins, and a gathering of relatives sitting cross-legged on woven mats, hands pressed together in prayer. Incense swirling lazily through the air, mixing with the scent of lemongrass and boiled chicken broth. Monks chanted blessings to mark the beginning of a new life. And somewhere in that small house, two teenagers—still blushing, still half-children—became husband and wife.

There weren't any grand vows or rehearsed declarations. But as Dad adjusted the gold chain around Mom's neck, something settled between them. A silent promise to stay together. To survive. To walk through whatever was coming next from this war, side by side.

WHAT WE BROUGHT ACROSS THE RIVER

Just weeks after their wedding, the deafening tension of the country was short lived. It finally broke when Pathet Lao announced the next steps after seizing full control of the government, now that the bloodshed was over. The country's new flag, red and blue with a single white disc in the middle, was hoisted over the capital. The days of elephants on our flag were no more. It marked the end of the monarchy, the end of American involvement to try and stop it, and the beginning of a regime that would swallow the country whole.

What had started as a teenage romance, sweet and awkward, was now caught in the sudden collapse of everything familiar. The same hands that had just exchanged lifelong commitment now had to carry fear and uncertainty of what would become of their country.

The joy of marriage quickly became shadowed by ambivalence. Friends and relatives continued to disappear around them without a word, family members separated without knowing if they were dead or alive—rumors of reeducation camps, arrests, executions continued. Villagers no longer spoke freely, and trust became a scarce resource. Even your own neighbors could report you for speaking against the Pathet Lao, so everyone kept to themselves. Every interaction carried weight. One wrong word could end everything.

Mom had always dreamed of raising children in the same village where she once played barefoot as a girl. But dreams were quickly replaced with hard decisions that were urgent, irreversible ones. They could no longer build a future in Laos. Not under this new rule.

Not with the aftermath thick in the air. And soon, my parents would join the growing swarm of families searching for escape routes.

They were children themselves when they were asked to become everything at once: spouses, survivors, parents, and refugees.

Much of Laos was already unrecognizable. Then came the promises—spoken through official mouths, dressed in the language of peace. The new Pathet Lao government urged those who had fled their villages in the early days of war to return to their original homes. Now that the war was over, they promised homes would be restored, land returned, and families reunited. It was a message soaked in promises, or what looked like promises to weary people.

For many, including Mom's family, they believed it was real. After years of living in Houayxay, Grandmother began to pack once more, preparing to return to their home in Luang Namtha. The very place Mom's father never returned to, the place they had fled in the beginning out of anguish.

But for my Mom, the idea of going back was not simply a change in geography—it was a reopening of old wounds that had never healed. The place where grief had first rooted itself in her life. And now, it was controlled by the very hands that had caused that grief. The government's promises, however sweetened, felt like tricks dressed in uniform. They were not bridges, they were bait. A symbol of the Lao people who remain, signifying their surrender and acceptance of the new government.

By then, she was married to Dad. And though she was still young, she had already learned to listen to her instincts. Stubbornly, she decided she would not go back with my grandmother and her siblings. Not to the village, not to fall victim to the regime, not to the radical government. Instead, she would remain in Houayxay at least for the time being, standing beside her new husband and his family, deciding what to do next instead of returning to the rubble of what had once been.

My grandmother was heartbroken. She had already buried so many parts of her past, now she would have to leave her daughter behind too. But when she looked into Mom's eyes, she saw a certainty she could not deny.

There was no arguing with it. With her voice trembling, she asked for only one thing: "Don't forget us. Come back to visit as often as you can." And so she turned away, gathered the rest of her children, and headed back to their home village of Luang Namtha, back to whatever was waiting for them.

Mom kept her promise. Once her family moved back, she endured the long and jarring bus rides to visit her siblings as often as she could. Each journey etched itself into her bones—two hours spent on winding roads, through dusty stretches of countryside that only made the ache of separation louder. The visits brought laughter, food, the closeness of family—but they were always shadowed by her knowledge that she would leave again. That goodbye was never really far from hello.

With every visit, it became clearer: the peace being sold was a performance. Dad's family could see it too. They understood what wasn't being said—the tightening rules, the sudden disappearances, the dull fear that threaded itself into daily life. Life in Laos had changed. You could feel it in your chest, in your breath, in the way neighbors avoided eye contact when walking past soldiers. The land seemed to speak more softly, like it knew it was being listened to.

Eventually, the question stopped being if Mom, Dad, and Dads family would leave Laos for good—but how. So they planned in secret. Carefully. Silently. Secrets passed among family members like smuggled currency. Escape meant risk, danger, possibly death—but staying meant surrender. And neither Mom nor Dad could see a future in surrender.

Before they finalized their plans to leave Laos, Mom took one last bus trip to see her family one more time. She knew what it meant. She knew it would likely be the final time she saw her siblings for an unknown amount of time, maybe if ever. Before they sat down for dinner, Mom pulled her eldest sister Chankham to the side, and let her know that she was leaving the country with her new husband and his family, the words caught in her throat. It wasn't just a confession, it was a goodbye woven into a prayer.

The sisters wept together. Their bodies collapsing into each other like pages in the same story, torn by different chapters. Mom begged her siblings to pack and come with them. But fear, always fear, held them back.

They would stay. They could not yet make that leap.

"Come with us, we can all start a new life. Aren't you tired of being afraid?" Mom pleaded with Chankham, but she shook her head. "We can't go. We have to accept this is the way things are now." She let go of Mom's hand. They joined their mother and the rest of their siblings for a warm meal and Mom tried to keep a straight face with her secret, as the chatter filled the room. Mom and Chankham exchanged solemn glances across the table.

When the bus pulled away for the final time back to Houayxay, Mom sat in her seat with tears stinging her eyes. Her heart ached with the weight of leaving. She watched the trees blur past, the green hills of Luang Namtha dissolving behind her.

It would be many long years before Mom ever returned to them. And during those years—through hunger, resettlement, motherhood, and the strangeness of starting over—she carried that question with her, tucked somewhere deep and painful: Did I abandon them… or did I save myself? There was no easy answer. Only a calm resolve. A knowing. That the kind of love it takes to leave isn't any smaller than the love it takes to stay. It's just lonelier.

I never knew what sunk in for her after that final goodbye. I only knew that my mother's voice sometimes wavered when she spoke about her siblings. Every once in a while, she would go mute in the middle of a chore, staring out the window like she was trying to see beyond it—across time, across countries, across the distance she had once chosen.

There were photographs she kept stowed away in old envelopes, and letters tucked into boxes, yellowing with age over the years but never thrown out.

Mom and Dad's life had been shaped by impossible choices. The decision to survive sometimes meant leaving, and love often looked like sacrifice. Every comfort I took for granted in America—every school lunch, every evening spent playing in the neighborhood street, every birthday party with store-bought cake—would cost my parents all the people they had left behind.

I didn't think much about exile as a kid, because I didn't see my parents as refugees. They never used that word. Instead, they spoke in more practical terms, about adjusting, about starting over, about what we had now. They didn't burden us with the weight of the past, not directly. But the past was always there. In the way Mom put money away to send back home. In the way Dad locked the doors each night with a double-check as if someone was still coming for them or the way they avoided speaking negatively about politics even in the U.S. They never talked about going back home to live, even when other relatives wrote letters asking when they would. Their past lived in what we didn't ask, in what they didn't say.

Together, they walked away from their entire world with each chapter to try and build a new one, brick by invisible brick. To start over with no blueprint. To carry both memory and guilt, both grief and gratitude. And now even decades later, the ache of those early decisions would spill through everything that came after.

    I wondered what it was like for my mother on that final bus ride. How did she feel so confident about their plans as she watched the hills of Luang Namtha fade into memory? Or if she already knew she would never be able to go back to who she was before. Because that very moment was about to divide her life into a before and an after.

    I try to piece together the story from fragments and old photos. Her decision to survive, to leave behind a place that no longer felt like home, was the reason I would eventually grow up in a country where I could freely ask these types of questions. That day, that bus ride didn't just carry her away from her village, it carried her toward the life she would soon create for us.

3 | The Refugee Camp

When Mom returned to Dad and his family in Houayxay, there was no room for delay. The promise of survival came with an expiration date, and they could feel it inching closer with every passing day. Their escape was quietly mapped out in whispers and shadows. Preparing themselves before the last threads of freedom were severed.

There was no time to barter or wait for fair offers. Dad's family let go of their home with barely a second thought. The house, once filled with memories and meals, was handed off for next to nothing. Time had become the only currency worth anything. And speed—unflinching, unforgiving—was everything.

The plan was split into two phases. The first wave would be Dad's father, uncle, and two older brothers. They would cross the Mekong River into Thailand. Their mission was to establish a foothold in Chiang Kham (Chang-Come), a quiet, faraway village tucked into the folds of Thailand's countryside. You wouldn't find it on most maps. But for them, it held the only direction left that pointed to safety.

The eldest men bore the most responsibility and the highest risk. If the first crossing failed, Dad's entire family wouldn't be at risk. If they succeeded, the rest of the family would have a place to land on the other side. It was a plan with no guarantees, but hope, folded into strategy.

It was a split marked by trust, born of necessity. The family fractured temporarily, like a river dividing into two streams, each carrying its own risk across the border winds.

There was one rare advantage, Dad's uncle had Thai ancestry. In a time when names and identities could mean life or death, that sliver of lineage was everything. His bloodline gave them access to what most could only dream of—land. In Chiang Kham, he was able to quietly purchase a modest home without drawing unwanted attention. A thin-walled house on unfamiliar land, but it was legal. It was hidden. It was theirs.

Back in Houayxay, Mom and Dad waited with his mother and grandmother—three generations suspended in time, watching the horizon and waiting for their signal. They spent their days preparing in silence, every movement underscored by worry. They packed essentials and rationed belongings, ready to flee at a moment's notice once word came that the crossing had been successful.

Their home was already spoken for. A Lao family who was too frightened to run, resigned to survive under the new regime and agreed to take it. Buyers were rare, but desperation was common. Across town, displaced families lingered like ghosts, looking for shelter among the ruins of what once was. Even if the walls whispered of another family's loss, they would live in them anyway. Because any walls were better than none.

When the signal finally came, it came through Dad's

uncle. The first phase had worked. The men were safe. A new home was waiting.

He had secured passage for the second group with a Thai boatman willing to take the risk. A stranger whose name they didn't know, whose face they wouldn't recognize. But he accepted the payment and named a time and place. A curve in the river. A stretch cloaked in darkness. No second chances.

It was a gamble, like everything else in war. But they had no choice left except to believe in the plan and in each other.

Everyone had heard the stories. Boatmen who betrayed families for a pouch of gold or a favor with the Pathet Lao. Men who smiled, took your money, then returned with soldiers instead of safe passage. In those days, survival hinged as much on luck as on trust and trust was in short supply.

Still, Mom and Dad believed this was their best option. Staying meant certainty of arrest, of reeducation, or a life of erasure. Leaving meant gambling everything on a stranger and a river that had swallowed too many before them.

Across the countryside, similar scenes played out in hushed, desperate repetition. Families disappeared one by one under moonlight, slipping through back doors and trails, led by men who claimed to know the jungle's secrets. Mercenaries, smugglers, and defectors all played roles in this silent exodus. Entire generations moved like spirits who were unseen, unheard, but unstoppable.

Lao escapees traveled only at night, hidden beneath

the thick canopy of jungle trees. When the daytime approached, they vanished into caves, or climbed high into branches to avoid patrols to wait til it was dark again. Their babies learned the sound of silence. Mothers muffled their cries and rocked them gently, whispering lullabies to keep them calm. With fear of being revealed while hiding.

For the Hmong, escape wasn't a dream—it was survival. The new regime had marked them as enemies. Soldiers swept through their villages with fire and bullets, burning homes and executing men accused of aiding the Americans. The war may have ended on paper, but the hunt for "traitors" raged on.

For those who made it to the banks of the Mekong River, they faced a different kind of trial. The water, calm on the surface, carried a quiet menace. It became the final dividing line between despair and possibility.

Some families paid for boats. Others cobbled together rafts from bamboo, rubber tires, or oil drums, anything that floated. They placed elders and children on top while the able-bodied swam alongside, pushing through the current, teeth chattering from cold, lungs burning from effort.

Those who tried to swim the river without a raft often disappeared beneath its surface, swept away by the current, or worse, spotted and shot by patrolling soldiers. Each crossing was a whispered prayer: that the river wouldn't take them, that bullets wouldn't find them, that the Thai border guards would show mercy.

Many didn't make it, getting caught before they ever

reached the water. Others vanished mid-crossing, their bodies claimed by the Mekong without a trace.

For those who reached the other side, they were barely breathing, trembling, soaked to the bone and freedom did not feel like triumph. Exhausted, feeling a sense of collapse. Abandoning relatives and their home land.

As Mom and Dad waited for their arranged date for the boat man to arrive, they successfully downsized. They shrank their life into what could be carried out quietly. Just small bundles of survival. Every night, they braced for the sound of a knock outside their door, hearts racing at each rustle in the dark. Fearful that someone had found out, that word spread they had sold their home to escape. Information given to the wrong person could destroy their chances.

They were part of a silent revolution now. Not the kind fought with weapons or flags, but with flight and the aching will to live. It wasn't heroism that pushed them forward. It was a passion for freedom. And the terrifying clarity that nothing would ever be the same again.

As part of their plan, they never wanted to register as refugees once they got to the other side. They had no intention of entering the sprawling refugee camps across the Thai border, even though they knew they existed. They already knew they didn't want to be seen as displaced, pitied, or caught in a system with no clear end.

Although the camps might have offered food and

shelter for Lao escapees, they also held limbo. Long lines. Barbed wire. Uncertainty. Instead, Mom and Dad dreamed of something simpler, quieter—a modest life hidden among the Thai people. They dreamed of waking up each day without fear, blending in, working hard, and maybe one day, calling it home. What they wanted was not safety as much as invisibility. Anonymity.

But even that hope required risk. To disappear quietly, they had to trust the boatman their uncle had hired. A stranger with no name, no promise, no reason to protect them. He was their one chance across the Mekong. One river. One crossing. And everything depended on him.

They packed two sets of clothes, a small sack of food, and a few irreplaceable keepsakes. Everything else—their wedding gifts, cooking pots, the faded photograph of Mom's father—they left behind. She couldn't bear to risk it. The photo of her father might connect her to him, a man the new regime accused of being a CIA informant years before. Though it wasn't true, it didn't matter. In this new Laos, suspicion was enough to cost you your life.

They left their remaining belongings to the family who had bought their home. It was the price they paid for time—for an exit. And that trade, unfair as it seemed, may have saved their lives.

When the date of escape finally came, they didn't sleep. They couldn't. They left Houayxay under the veil of moonlight, their footsteps barely disturbing the dirt path beneath them. The air was cool and damp, the kind of cold that sank deep into bone and stayed there. Every sound felt amplified: an insect's chirp, a dog barking in the distance, the rustle of wind in the trees. Each one rang out like the night itself was listening.

Without flashlights, they navigated by starlight and moonshine, their eyes slowly adjusting to the dark. Every movement was measured. Every breath counted.

They reached the edge of the Mekong at 3:00 a.m. The river was intimidating, stretching before them like a black ribbon in motion, wide and quietly menacing. Moonlight bounced off the surface like a blade's reflection. There were no trees here, no shelter, just an open bank. Feeling exposed, they crept back several feet into the brush, crouching low, cloaked in nerves and cold sweat. They would wait until the boatman arrived.

The waiting was the worst part. Every snapped twig made them flinch. Every subtle thump could have been the footfall of a soldier. When a distant voice rang out behind them, time seemed to stop. Were they being followed? But it occurred to them, there were others nearby who were running too.

They didn't speak to each other. Just exchanged glances with tight, wordless flashes of trust and fear. Questions they didn't dare ask aloud. Mom had hoped others wouldn't attempt to get on their boat, leaving them to fend for themselves.

Her mind wandered in spirals. She thought of her mother, her sisters, the smell of steamed bamboo and grilled river fish. She hadn't said a proper goodbye. Only to Chankham. There had been no time, and now that chapter of her life was closing without ceremony. The ache of guilt was sharp, but it was overtaken by something else: resolve. They had come this far, there was no turning back now.

Then came the sound of salvation: the creak of oars cutting through water, faint but unmistakable. Her chest tightened.

From the shadows, a boat appeared—long and narrow—gliding toward the riverbank with a quiet grace. A man stood at the helm, hunched, wearing a wide hat that nearly covered his eyes. His oar moved in slow rhythm, patient and practiced. As he neared the shore, he whispered a name—Dad's last name—barely audible above the lapping water.

Dad nodded. It was the signal. There was no time for hesitation. They revealed themselves from the brush and boarded quickly. She worried about how loud they were as the boat rocked beneath them, slick with damp. The man pulled back a canvas tarp and motioned for them to crouch beneath it. It reeked of mildew and river mud. They obeyed without question, pressing their bodies together in the cramped space as darkness swallowed them whole.

Mom's hands trembled as she clutched the collar of her shirt. She reached for the tiny Buddha pendant she wore and whispered a prayer to herself. Was this man truly here to help? Or was this the moment of betrayal? She thought of her father, how he hadn't been careful enough, how it had cost him his life.

The boat began to move. Clumsy at first, then steady. Each stroke of the oar sounded like a heartbeat in the water. They didn't speak. They didn't move. Even breathing felt dangerous.

Under the tarp, Mom could hear the river lapping against the wooden sides. She could feel Dad's hand on her shoulder, still and grounding. A quiet promise that she wasn't alone.

Minutes passed. Then more. Time lost its shape. The boat began to feel like it was moving sideways, rather than forward. The other side of the river still felt impossibly far.

With her sight masked by darkness under the tarp, her other senses sharpened. She listened, trying to track the boat's motion, feeling every shift beneath her. Her toes went numb, submerged in the cold water that had pooled at the bottom. She heard voices outside the tarp, boat men on other boats, muffled and hard to make out. She froze like stone. She was sure their boat would be stopped. She was sure this could be their last moment alive. That their story could end right here, leaving them executed on the river, her family in Luang Namtha never knowing her whereabouts.

But to her surprise, the boat slowed and came to a stop. The wood scraped softly against mud. The boatman lifted the tarp and gestured for them to go. For a moment, no one moved. He urged them to get off board immediately, sensing he was just as scared of being caught.

They rose, legs stiff, hearts pounding. As Mom

stepped onto the muddy bank, lunging forward, the earth clung to her shoes like hands trying to pull her back. They looked up and saw a road, the climb to the road above was steep. They had to crawl to get up there, clawing at the hillside with bare hands and soaked feet. Mud caked their arms and knees, but still they climbed, driven by fear and urgency. As if the past itself was chasing them.

At the top of the road, a car waited. Inside sat another man—another stranger to trust. He said nothing, just held out a hand toward Dad.

Dad reached into his shirt pocket and handed over a folded scrap of paper, an address scribbled in Lao. A brief exchange of glances passed between the two men, and the driver nodded once, the unspoken language of survival needing no translation. The engine sputtered to life, and the car jerked forward.

For three long hours, they rumbled along narrow, unpaved roads through the remote Thai countryside. The landscape blurred past: mist-covered trees, distant rice fields, scattered homes still asleep. Mom sat in silence, eyes fixed on the horizon, unable to rest. The border was behind them, but her body didn't catch up yet.

The rising sun poured soft light over the hills, but it didn't feel like a peaceful morning. It felt like exposure. Like danger was still following close behind. She kept waiting for a voice to call out, for soldiers to appear and drag them back. But no one came.

Instead, something else arrived—a slow, quiet

realization. A soft shift inside her. They would never turn back. Tears slipped from her eyes, not from fear this time, but from the weight of release.

When the car finally stopped in front of a modest home tucked in the green hills of Chiang Kham, Mom stepped out and felt it: not joy, not quite. But something close. A loosening. A breath that reached deeper than it had in years.

She looked around at the stillness of this unfamiliar place and, for the first time in a long time, exhaled without fear. They had made it. Thailand was now their home. They were safe.

Chiang Kham was a small, unremarkable town hidden in the hills of northern Thailand. It was the kind of place easily missed if you weren't looking. There were no flashing signs, no promises of prosperity, just winding country roads and the hush of a discreet life, surrounded by neighbors they didn't know. But for Mom and Dad, it was more than enough.

After all they had endured—the war, the betrayal, the escape—this quiet town felt like a soft landing. It wasn't a destination, it was a beginning. A place where survival could take root and become something steadier.

They settled into a modest house overlooking rice fields and banana trees, secured through the efforts of Dad's uncle, who had paved the way for them. Their new life didn't begin with dreams, it began with necessity. They planted themselves in new soil and hoped, with time, they could grow.

Thai wasn't a foreign tongue. As children, both Mom

and Dad had studied it in school and tucked it away like a second skin they never imagined they'd need. Now it returned to them, halting but familiar, like a melody half-remembered. They relearned how to speak, not just in language, but in the unspoken grammar of daily life. Careful, deliberate, cautious. Survival didn't always require words, but it demanded awareness.

Dad took whatever work he could find with pay under the table. He spent long, grueling days in the fields—hauling, hammering, lifting until his shoulders ached and his palms cracked open. It was a far cry from his earlier years spent as a young monk. Each evening, he returned home coated in sweat and dust, the scent of earth lingering on his skin.

Mom remained behind with his mother and grandmother, gradually finding her footing in this new life. She was still so young—barely a wife, now a daughter-in-law—still learning the shape of a traditional woman through daily practice. The kitchen became her classroom. With quiet humility, she learned to cook beside them. They made northern Thai curries, cooked with fermented fish pastes, and fiery chili dips pounded by hand in stone mortars. She learned to prepare sticky rice just right, to adjust the flavors of dishes by taste and instinct. Every meal became a small triumph, every recipe a step toward becoming.

Though she didn't know when or how their family would grow, she was already preparing for it. These early days, shaped by hard work and adaptation, would become the foundation for the life she was slowly beginning to imagine.

But it wasn't long before Mom found out she was pregnant with their first child. She was full of a mix of joy and nerves. Mom was happy that their first child would be born on a safer land, away from the dangers of Laos. Thailand offered a little bit of that security, that's what kept them moving forward. During her pregnancy, she tried to perfect the dishes she learned, so she could be a more capable mom. Dad worked harder, spent more hours in the fields or on surrounding farms, to prepare for the baby's arrival.

By the time Mom was in her final trimester of pregnancy, she was still doing chores and contributing to the household. One afternoon, she was out in the rice field, the sun hot on her back as she bent low to pluck and chop the rice stalks. She didn't intend to stay out for too long, she'd return home once she gathered the rice. But the day turned against her. Her foot slipped in the thick wet mud and before she could steady herself, she fell, the weight of her pregnant belly crashing onto the ground, her body pressing into the earth.

Panicked, she stumbled back to the house, muddy and shaken. Dad's mom cleaned her up and she rested for the remainder of the afternoon. But as the day passed, something in her gut told her what she was trying to deny: the baby wasn't moving anymore. And the quiet inside her belly was the most terrifying feeling in the world. Soon, the sharp pains followed.

When Dad took her to the small local hospital in

Chiang Kham, they were met with indifference. With no money or proper paperwork, they became an afterthought in a place where locals took precedence.

Dad begged, pleaded with the staff to help her, but she was left waiting in unbearable pain, her body heavy with fear. Around her, she noticed the hospital was ill equipped, it had little to no machines to monitor her. She was just a woman in a bed, forgotten by the world around her.

Eventually, the staff tended to her and told her it was time to push. She was afraid to do it, but there was no other choice. Every part of her was desperate to bring the baby out alive. The pain had already stretched for a few days now, from the moment she fell to this moment in the hospital. So she pushed with every ounce of strength she had left, until the head finally emerged, and the midwife helped pull the baby from her. But there was no cry. Just silence. The baby's skin was blue, lifeless.

In that moment, a deep, wretched pain took root in her chest. She didn't even recognize the sound that tore from her throat, a cry so raw, so full of despair, it felt like the world had crumbled inside of her. It was a boy. Their son. And he was gone.

The days that followed were like a fog, a blur of physical recovery that could never touch what was breaking inside her. While Dad made arrangements with neighbors to bury their son in a simple, unmarked grave, something heavy pressed between them, leaving them both speechless. They couldn't afford a proper funeral, so there would be no ceremony, no mark of his life, just the empty space where their dreams once lived.

The grief they shared was too deep for words, too vast to fully process. They were young, barely equipped to handle such a loss, and it came so quickly, so violently, it almost shattered them. The silence between them grew, heavy and thick, and for a while, it felt like the whole world had paused, leaving them suspended in the weight of something too horrible to understand.

They had escaped the war, but nothing could have prepared them for this. In a slow and painful movement of time, they shifted their focus on what to do next.

It was inevitable. Being stateless in Thailand meant living with nothing but disadvantages. In Chiang Kham, they were safe, but not seen. They had no identification, no papers to prove who they were or where they belonged. They were ghosts in the system—present in body, invisible on record. And while their neighbors welcomed them with kindness, their presence came with boundaries: no right to formal work, no access to government services, no real claim to the soil beneath their feet.

For a while, they endured. They were young and devoted to each other, and for a time, that was enough. But as months turned to years, the ache for something more began to grow—stability, opportunity, a real future. Chiang Kham's peace slowly began to feel like a ceiling. Two years passed. And in that quiet, the dream of building a lasting life there began to dim under the weight of reality. If they stayed, there would be no schools for their future children. No pathway out of poverty. No chance to become anything more than what they already were—grateful, but stuck.

Eventually, they packed again and tried once more. This time Mom and Dad brought Dad's grandmother with them and moved north to Mae Sai (Mahhs-Eye). It was a pulsing border town where Thailand brushed against Myanmar. Life in Mae Sai was loud, messy, and alive. Markets spilled into the streets, motorbikes weaved through narrow alleys, and the scent of grilled meats and jasmine rice filled the humid air. In a place built on movement and trade, anonymity had value. They believed they could disappear into the rhythm of the town by finding work, finding shelter, maybe even a future.

Dad took more odd jobs wherever he could—hauling cargo, fixing motors, working in crowded street markets. There were no guarantees, only day-by-day survival. The hours were long, the pay meager. Still, he worked. Still, he returned each evening with aching feet and silent resolve.

Mom adapted too, sewing when there was fabric to sew, bartering when there was something to trade, always stretching what little they had into something that could feed them another day.

But the truth never loosened its grip: they had no legal names in this country. No birth certificates. No identification cards. The weight of statelessness wrapped around them like a shroud. It was more than limiting—it was erasing. They lived on the edge of everything, grateful to be alive but aching to belong.

It was in Mae Sai that Mom gave birth to another child. A daughter they named Saeng, meaning "light" or "radiance." Her arrival was like the sun rising over a field scorched by too many losses. After the heartbreak of losing their first son, Saeng was a flicker of hope. In her, they poured every ounce of love they had carried through years of grief and longing. She was proof that something new and beautiful could still grow from the ashes of all they had endured.

But joy doesn't erase the hardship. Their reality remained unforgiving. Food grew scarce. Dad's income could no longer stretch to feed four mouths. And then, an unexpected loss arrived like a final blow. Dad's grandmother passed away right there with them in Mai Sai.

She had been their constant, a living thread to the past, the oldest witness to their journey. She had survived colonization, war, revolution, and exile. She was there the night they crossed the Mekong together. Her death wasn't just personal, it was ancestral. It marked the end of an era, a rupture in the lineage that no words could fill.

Grief, fatigue, and dwindling resources forced them to return to Chiang Kham with their new baby girl. But they returned changed. Not the same wide-eyed couple seeking refuge, but parents, mourners, and survivors once more. They brought more than just their belongings, they carried the heaviness of dreams deferred, of a grandmother lost, and of a world that still had no place for them. But with Saeng now in the fold, it was a reminder that the story wasn't over. That something bright had been born in the dark.

Even among familiar faces back in Chiang Kham, they were left to ask the same question they had asked too many times before: what now?

With an illegal status, no steady income, and a child to raise, they were surviving—but surviving was not the same as living. They were caught in a kind of bureaucratic purgatory, drifting without direction. The years stretched out ahead of them like a road with no exit, paved with uncertainty and longing for a place to belong.

Dad's other uncle, Uncle Lue, gave them a glimmer of possibility. The name of a place that had once sounded like their last resort: the refugee camp in Chiang Khong (Chang-Kong).

Officially, it was known as the Chiang Khong Baan Tong Refugee Camp, one of many refugee camps scattered along Thailand's northern border. For some of the Lao people, it was a waiting room. For others, it was a dead end. But for Mom, the question of going was one she could no longer ignore.

She didn't want to go, it was never part of their plan when they got there. But Mom knew given their circumstances, they might have no other choice. The word 'camp' brought up stories she'd tried to forget—of fences and ration lines, of confinement and despair. And yet, they had reached their limit and exhausted every other option.

Mom knew they could no longer keep living their lives this way. So one hot afternoon, with the sun bearing down like judgment, she boarded a bus headed for Chiang Khong to see Uncle Lue and find out more. She sat alone, the engine's low rumble blending with the rhythm of her thoughts, each mile blurring the lines between fear and determination.

When she arrived at Uncle Lue's house, she was met with nothing. The windows were shuttered. The air was still. The village dogs did not bark. She stood on the porch for a long moment, unsure whether to knock again or turn around. Lue was not home, but something inside her refused to get back on the bus to leave back to Chiang Kham without answers. She remembered him saying the camp was near his home. So she stepped off his porch, her shoes scraped the dirt as she headed back toward the village, setting off on foot.

The heat was suffocating. Dust rose with every step, coating her legs, stinging her eyes. The village unfolded around her slowly—small wooden homes, faded laundry swaying on lines, the scent of fried garlic through the air. Life carried on all around her, but her search made her feel desperate.

And then, almost by accident, after walking aimlessly she came upon it. A tall fence loomed ahead, stretching long and sharp around the perimeter of a vast compound. Barbed wire crowned its top like a warning. Thai soldiers stood at the intervals, their rifles slung casually but unmistakably over their shoulders. This had to be it. The metal gate was closed, its surface dull with rust, the only movement seen coming from the occasional flash of cloth as people shuffled behind the fence.

Her heart began to pound. This didn't look like a sanctuary. It looked like a cage. Like the reeducation camps she had heard rumors of back in Laos—places where men vanished, and families were broken apart in the name of control. She desired something gentler, but what she saw unsettled her. Was this really safe? Was this what freedom looked like?

She considered asking the guards at the gate, but fear held her tongue. What if they questioned her? What if they asked for documents she didn't have, piecing together the truth—that she and Dad had been living illegally in Thailand all this time, undocumented and unregistered? A single wrong word could unravel everything. The wrong face could recognize her. The wrong question could send her back into the shadows, or worse.

So she walked, slowly, carefully, keeping her eyes low. She let herself blend in, passing as just another Thai local weaving through the marketplace nearby. She hoped that no one would look at her too closely. That her clothes, her posture, and the way she carried herself would be enough disguise.

As she moved to an area out of the soldier's view, a different sound reached her ears—one that didn't match the gloom of guard towers and watchful eyes. It was the sound of life. Bartering voices closeby: women exchanging bundles of morning glory greens for coins, children laughing as they played with sticks, the rhythmic thump of knives chopping vegetables on wooden boards. There, along the fence's edge, a kind of makeshift market had formed. A liminal space where the inside and outside met but could never quite touch between the fence of the camp.

Lao refugees stood behind the fence, holding up handmade goods and bags of produce they grew on the compound. On the other side of the fence, Thai villagers stood, exchanging money through narrow openings. It was beautiful, a sense of community, a life trying to bloom in the spaces left by displacement. Commerce, connection, even laughter—none of it erased the separation, but it softened it.

Mom stood frozen, watching. Just on the other side of those bars was a world that mirrored hers: people who were just like her, speaking her language, who carried the same memories of river crossings and had vanished fathers too.

She didn't know how long she stood there, pressed into the shadows, watching this strange choreography of resilience and desperation. And just as she began to step away, unsure if this was the answer or another dead end,

"Seetong? Is that you?" The voice sliced through the still air.

She turned, startled. Her body tensed. There, through the fence, a woman was waving. Mom squinted into the sun, blinking past the brightness. And then she saw her: a face she hadn't expected, someone from her old life. A connection to what once was.

At that moment, her faith returned. The worry and ache of not knowing loosened its grip, just enough. Mom stepped closer, Her eyes scanned the fence until they landed with certainty on her friend in between the opening of the rails. She was holding a sleeping newborn in a faded cloth sling. Her voice caught in her throat.

"Yes," she said with uncertainty, not quite believing it herself. "It's me."

Mom blinked in disbelief, the sun in her eyes making the old friend before her seem almost like a mirage.

"Khammee?" she said, voice cracking with surprise.

The woman grinned, stepping closer. "Seetong! It is you!" she laughed, her voice carrying the same warmth it had back when they were just schoolgirls in Houayxay, before the war had carved so much distance between who they were and who they had become. "What are you doing here?"

Mom's heart swelled. There, behind the fence of a refugee camp in Chiang Khong, stood one of her dearest friends—Khammee, alive and safe, yet behind a wall she could not cross. They had not seen each other since their days in school, and yet it felt like no time had passed.

Mom leaned toward the narrow opening in the fence, lowering her voice as she explained how she and Dad had crossed the Mekong River, how they had lived discreetly in Thailand, unseen, and how she had come now only to understand what life might look like on the inside.

Khammee's smile softened, her brows knitting in concern. "You have to be careful," she warned. "You won't get through the front gate without the right story. They're watching for people like us—refugees, yes, but only the newly arrived ones. You've been in Thailand all this time and haven't registered as a refugee."

She gestured for Mom to follow her around the edge of the camp to a more secluded spot where the noise of trade and barter muffled their voices. There, tucked between low brush and rusted wire, was a small break in the fence—just enough for two women to lean in close and speak without fear.

"That's where I stay," Khammee said, pointing toward a modest shack just behind her beyond the fence line. "We built it ourselves with sticks, tarps, anything we could find. Dirt floor. No doors. But it's better than nothing. At least here, we can breathe."

Mom followed her friend's finger with her eyes, her gaze sweeping across the camp. It looked like a makeshift village stitched together from scraps of survival. The huts stood shoulder to shoulder like fragile dominoes, patched with bamboo and plastic. Smoke from wood stoves spiraled into the sky. Women bent over washbasins. Men dragged fallen limbs for firewood. Children raced through narrow dirt alleys, barefoot and laughing, their joy unbroken by the wire fencing around them.

There was sorrow in the sight, it made Mom sad to see her people there trying to make the camp a home. But there was also something else, something softer.ABdignity, perhaps. Or endurance.

Mom's voice lowered when she finally asked, "How do they treat you in there?" The question hung in the air, heavy with history. Reeducation camps. Disappearances. The cold logic of power back in Laos.

But Khammee shook her head. "This isn't like that," she said gently. "This isn't Laos. No one's trying to break us here. We're not prisoners. We're all waiting for something better. That's all."

The answer landed in Mom's chest with a strange, aching relief. She exhaled slowly, unsure whether to believe it, but needing to. "How do we get in?" she asked.

Khammee hesitated, glancing toward the guards in the distance. "Well, it's not going to be easy. You have to tell them you just got here. Last night. That you crossed the river and came straight here."

She paused, her voice dropping. "Come tomorrow. Bring your husband. Bring your daughter. You'll have a better chance if they see you as one unit. Don't wait too long. They turn people away if they think they're lying."

Mom felt the ground shift beneath her, the weight of the decision forming like storm clouds in her mind. But Khammee smiled softly, reaching a hand through the fence. "If you come back," she said, brushing Mom's hand lightly, "I'll be here."

The ride back to their home in Chiang Kham felt different than all the bus rides Mom took before. The countryside still passed by in a blur of the farms and tired sky. But her thoughts were locked on the camp—on the children's bare feet, the huts lined like old village homes, and the small break in the fence where a new life had revealed itself.

When Mom shared what she'd seen with Dad's family, and what Khammee said about the compound, their reaction was swift and full of doubt.
"We're doing fine here," they said. "Why go looking for more uncertainty? We have a roof. We have peace."

Dad's family meant well, but Mom heard something else underneath their words: fear. The kind of fear that builds walls around hope, that turns possibility into a threat. "Go," they told her, reluctantly. "You can take your husband, but leave Saeng with us. She'll be safe here."

But the thought stopped Mom cold. The suggestion repeated loudly in her memory. She remembered the day she left her own mother in Houayxay, the parting with Chankham in Luang Namtha. Of the years that followed, filled with shedding herself from more family members. But mostly, of the son they had lost the first time she became pregnant. She would not lose another child. "No," she said firmly. "We go together. If we're going to risk this, we do it as a family."

The next morning, with the sunrise just beginning to

light the sky, Mom and Dad gathered their few belongings, wrapped Saeng close to Mom's chest, and returned to Chiang Khong Baan Tong Refugee Camp.

Dad's family stayed behind, and in that moment, another branch of their lives fell away. And just like that, after Mom's family in Laos, now it was Dad's family in Chiang Kham refusing the same. With each decision, their family unit grew smaller, but also more focused. Mom and Dad chose each other each time. And that had to be enough.

At the camp, Mom did exactly as Khammee had instructed. She told the guards they had arrived the night before, weary from the river. She held Saeng close, trying not to look afraid. The Thai interviewers asked questions, noted their answers, and collected everything from them—every coin, every bit of jewelry, every token of value. "It will be returned," they said. But Mom was skeptical, she learned promises didn't mean much in times like this.

They were placed in a holding area—a long, narrow building nearby with concrete floors and no privacy. There were dozens of other families just like them, suspended in limbo. The days were sweltering hot within those walls and the nights were long and cold, with the unrelenting air that was thick with the smell of sweat and stale rice. Saeng whimpered in her sleep. Mom sang gentle lullabies she barely remembered.

Twenty-seven long days passed in that holding area like a lifetime. They had no way of knowing if they'd be accepted into the camp or sent back across the river to

Laos. Hope flickered and faded, reignited only by small mercies: a shared bowl of soup, a friendly smile from a fellow mother, the steady presence of Dad, who never once left Mom's side.

And the morning finally came, when their names were called. Mom lifted Saeng into her arms. Dad shouldered their bag. Together, they stepped forward, through the gate, past the fence, and into the refugee camp. It wasn't freedom. Not yet. But it was what looked like a start. A fragile, hard-won beginning they would build on, with patience, with the deep care and love that had carried them this far.

When Mom and Dad finally stepped past the gates of Chiang Khong Baan Tong, they entered more than a refugee camp, they entered a liminal world. A place not quite past, not yet future. A space between survival and the unknown.

The Chiang Kong camp had been originally designed for just 2,000 people. But the Mekong River kept bringing more each day. Escapees came in waves—some on boats, some on foot, many carrying nothing but the memory of what they left behind. The camp ballooned overnight, bursting at its seams.

Just north of it, the Chiang Saen camp had once served as a temporary refuge, a way station for those waiting on Chiang Khong's completion. At Chiang Saen, each refugee was given five baht's worth of food a day which included some rice, some cabbage, and a rare bit of meat. In the cold season, a single blanket was distributed per family. It wasn't much, but it was something. Survival came in small portions. But the truth was, many never made it out of Chiang Saen. By the time Chiang Khong finished building and opened its gates, the place was already full. Still, they kept coming.

Conditions inside the camps varied depending on the day, the donations, the politics of the hour. But the struggles were constant—malaria, cholera, ration lines that stretched into the dust, and the daily arithmetic of making enough food stretch far enough.

Aid and resources came mostly through the United Nations High Commissioner for Refugees, sometimes accompanied by church groups tied to the Red Cross.

At Chiang Khong, Mom and Dad did what they'd always done: they adapted. Each family was in charge of building their own shelter with whatever materials they could scavenge from the forest nearby. Finding any straw that was left, was gold. They used it for everything from roofs to walls, sleeping mats, and insulation. Dad cut down bamboo and carried it back on his shoulder while Mom wove it into walls. Saeng was still small then, strapped to Mom's back, her little fingers clinging to fabric, her eyes wide.

Every family had chores. Food distribution was run like clockwork as loudspeakers called out group numbers, and the camp lined up in the dust. Fish, pork, and bags of rice arrived with the occasional burst of generosity from American organizations. I'm not certain why, but it made me wonder if their aid came from the guilt of our defeat in the U.S. CIA's Secret War.

Thai villagers stood at the camp's edge trading and

buying fresh produce like green papaya, chilies, bundles of morning glory. It was strange, how Mom now stood inside the fence where she once lingered outside, watching.

Somehow, life began again. Inside the camp's walls, communities began to form. Women shared recipes passed down from vanished kitchens. Men worked together, cutting grass, fixing roofs, watching one another's children. It was a kind of village that was fragile, impermanent, but real.

There was a lot of loss living in the camp, she watched fragile children and elders get sick. Some of them died from the conditions there. Families who were worried sick with each pressing day, as they were barely holding on. She remembered seeing a pregnant woman, knowing her fate, that she might have to give birth right there behind those walls. Groups shared food with her, trying to keep her strong.

At night, the camp grew quieter, shadows stretched long under the dim bulbs strung between huts. Mom remembers those evenings most, the way people gathered to share stories. There were stories of escapes through jungles, of families separated by rivers and borders, of loved ones who vanished. Some stories were haunting, full of sorrow and loss. Others shimmered with improbable hope. Some were still looking for family members they got separated with on their journey. In those stories, they stitched together a sense of belonging, shared grief becoming shared strength. Either way, it was nice to be able to openly speak about their experiences in a safe place now.

And in those moments, Mom felt something she hadn't in a long time: security. Even if they lacked an abundance of material things. Even if they lacked any certainty. They were in a place where there would be no more pretending or hiding. Here, they could say they were Lao. Here, the truth didn't need to be buried.

But beyond the fence, the world debated what to do with them. The refugee crisis unfolding across Southeast Asia had reached the desks of diplomats oceans away. In the U.S., Congress argued over whether to allow 11,000 Lao refugees into the country, a number that barely scratched the surface of those waiting in camps across Thailand. Skeptics feared the cost, the cultural clash, the long shadow of responsibility. What would happen to these refugees, they asked, once they arrived? Would they be able to adapt? Would they survive in a country where everything—language, weather, and customs—would feel like another planet?

Meanwhile, Thailand was running out of room. They couldn't grant land to refugees without displacing their very own Thai citizens. And allowing permanent settlement would risk angering their communist neighbors. The camps were never meant to be a permanent home. They were a waiting room, a holding pen, a place to pass the time until a decision came from somewhere else.

Then, another fear took over, what if Eisenhower's Domino Theory would take into effect? Now that Laos has been taken over, the result should mean Thailand is next for communist takeover. Thailand was doing everything they could to protect and preserve their country. They assisted in the protection of Lao refugees as a public statement, that they will not fall to the regime.

Mom and Dad had once dreamed of becoming Thai citizens, of staying hidden, to be safe in a place that felt close to home. But that door had slowly closed. Their only option now was resettling even further from where they imagined.

Each family in the camp was asked to fill out a form listing two countries they would be willing to start over in. Mom and Dad selected France first, and the United States second.

When I asked Mom why she chose France, she couldn't remember her logic. Maybe they had heard rumors of better opportunities, or maybe they were just guessing, and anywhere would be better than where they were now. What mattered was the dream that somewhere across the ocean, there might be a place where Saeng could grow up without fear.

And so they waited again. Days turned into weeks. Weeks into several months. Every morning, the loudspeaker crackled to life, calling out names of families chosen for resettlement to countries they selected on their forms. Some cheered. Some cried. Some families were divided, one getting accepted into one country, while another was accepted to a different one. Oddly enough some didn't even want to leave the familiarity of the camp, even with all its hardships.

WHAT WE BROUGHT ACROSS THE RIVER

It was strange how quickly something so bare could become a kind of home. Mom and Dad never let themselves expect too much. But they watched, every morning, and listened intently to every name.

And then—on a hot, humid day in late January—everything changed forever. It was January 23, 1980. The sky stood at high noon over the camp. People milled about, already wilting in the heat. When the loud speaker clicked just as it did all the days before, but this time announcing a familiar name. Dad's name. Had they heard it right? They turned to look at each other, waiting for confirmation. The speakers repeated it again. It was true. They were chosen.

Everything flashed before them. Fleeing across the Mekong River, impersonating as Thai natives in Chiang Kham, the loss of their first born son, Saeng's birth in Mae Sai, and spending one year behind the fence of Chiang Kong Refugee Camp. With nothing but faith and each other, they were finally chosen. Their names were on the list. Their new destination: America. Not Thailand. Not Laos. Not even France. A new home and a place where a new kind of life could begin.

AMBER D. INTHAVONG

4 | AMERICA, JAN 23, 1980

Mom and Dad set off for America with almost nothing but a soft-sided bag, a few folded documents, and a baby girl barely old enough to remember the world they were leaving behind.

Everything happened so quickly, it hardly felt real. One moment, they were living behind a barbed wire fence in Chiang Khong, waiting for their names to be called. The next, they were ushered onto a bus heading south toward Bangkok, toward something unknown and irreversible.

The city buzzed with motion. Refugees moved through it like a restless tide, coming and going, too fast to fully see or follow. There wasn't time to think or breathe, only to follow and push forward. Always forward.

In Bangkok, they were funneled through health screenings in long, winding lines. The hallways were bare and bright, echoing with footsteps and quiet voices. Mom held Saeng on one hip, clutching their paperwork in the other hand with forms covered in English she couldn't read. She remembers the anxious energy filling the air, the shuffle of tired feet, the tension and urgency of it all.

They were surrounded by strangers, each one suspended in the same in-between space. There was no comfort, but there was a kind of unity. A silent understanding passed between eyes that met briefly, and then moved on. No one knew what would happen next, but they waited—for the results, for the stamps, for the green light that meant a new beginning.

They spent three nights in holding rooms, sleeping in shifts, trying to quiet the nerves that stretched thin with each passing hour. No one explained much. Just instructions. Sit here. Stand now. Walk this way. Sign this. There was no cruelty, but there was no gentleness either. Just efficiency. There were far too many people to treat with any tenderness.

Before leaving, someone handed them a manila envelope filled with official documents they couldn't understand, stamped and typed in a language that didn't yet belong to them.

Inside was everything from their flight itinerary, their relocation paperwork, and a name written in black ink: **R. Hanson**. A stranger who would meet them on the other side.

Mom had never heard of Seattle, Washington. She didn't know what it looked like, how the weather was, or how the people would be there. But when she filled out her resettlement form back in the camp, she had ticked the box for "United States" as her second choice. And the fact that she got what she asked for was enough. She was grateful.

Sometimes, she wondered what might've happened if they had been sent to France instead. Would they have spoken French at home? Would her children grow up sipping coffee in cafés and quoting poems in Parisian accents?

I wonder about that too sometimes, how one ticked box on a form could've rerouted our entire lives. But it wasn't France. It was America.

At the Bangkok airport, Dad exchanged the last of their Thai baht for ten U.S. dollars. It was a soft green bill, foreign and unfamiliar in his hands. It was all the money they had left. Their only luggage was that same bag they'd carried for years. The one that crossed borders, survived boats, checkpoints, and long journeys. At that point, it felt less like a bag and more like part of them. It was the one constant through everything they'd endured, even if they had little else to show for it.

The flight over the Pacific Ocean was long. Too long to count in hours. It was a big journey for their first time flying. Mom's hands stayed clenched around the armrest through every bump of turbulence. She stared out the window with a mix of awe and fear, watching the clouds stretch endlessly below them. The anxiety that once filled her as they crossed the Mekong now took a new shape. Back then, Laos had been terrifying because of what they were running from. America was terrifying because of everything they didn't yet know.

In Thailand they knew the language, the food and the terrain was similar. In America, everything would be foreign. The faces. The laws. The weather. Even the silence would sound different.

There she was, moving further away from her family. Putting more borders and miles between her, her siblings and her mother.

WHAT WE BROUGHT ACROSS THE RIVER

Still, under all the unknown, something else lived—a quiet flicker of possibility. A sense that maybe, just maybe, the world was opening up instead of closing in.

Over the roar of the engines, they reminded each other this would all be worth it. They passed Saeng between them when she cried. They leaned into the promise they'd made to each other, that all the chaos, the hunger, the aching goodbyes was leading them to this moment. Suspended in the sky, between two lives. Between the world they had known and the one they were still hoping for.

When their plane touched down in Washington State, it was early morning. The air outside the terminal was cool and damp, touched with the scent of rain and pine. The evergreens lined the distance like quiet sentinels—stoic, unmoving, timeless. The sky hung low, draped in thick gray clouds. It was nothing like the golden haze of Laos or the smoky brightness of Thai mornings.

Mom held Saeng close against her chest, her arms tired but firm. They stepped through the glass doors of the airport and into something new. A different world. A different life.

Near the baggage claim stood a man and a woman. The woman holding a sign with Dad's last name printed in bold letters. The same name that had once been whispered across the Mekong River, spoken over loudspeakers in the refugee camp, and scribbled onto forms they couldn't read. It stood on paper again, waiting for them. Mom and Dad had a hard time recognizing it, they weren't accustomed to seeing it written in English before. Luckily, the sign had **R. Hanson** written right below it. Mom held her envelope up to study it closer and compare. When Mr. Hanson approached them to help, he nodded with confirmation and shook Dad's hand.

Mr. Hanson was tall and bald, with kind eyes and an easy smile. His wife stood beside him, bundled in a thick coat. They looked like people from a distant world, clean and composed. But when they said, "Welcome home," something inside Mom softened. She didn't understand the words. But she understood the warmth. That part was universal.

The Hansons helped them load their one tattered bag into the back of a modest car and drove them through winding roads that seemed pulled from a dream. The forests rushed past in deep green blurs, the earth blanketed in moss, the houses tucked quietly among trees like hidden storybook cabins. It was nothing like they'd seen before.

There were no rice fields. No thatched roofs or ancient temples. Just pine trees, clean roads, and more cars than she could count.

Mom and Dad stared through the window in silence, watching the world blur by. Even the small houses looked enormous. Neatly trimmed lawns. Porches. Shiny glass windows without cracks. Two stories. Chimneys. Everything looked new. Untouched. Like something out of a movie she hadn't seen yet.

Later, they would learn the Hansons were not rich.

Just a middle-class American family that was kind, practical, generous. But to a young couple arriving with nothing but a baby and a small bag, it felt like they had landed inside someone else's dream.

That night, the Hansons gave them a small spare bedroom. Inside were two clean beds, soft blankets, and a place to unpack the little belongings they had brought with them. The room smelled faintly of cedar and laundry detergent, a scent Mom would come to associate with safety.

Mom sat on the edge of the bed, quiet for a long time. The stillness was almost too much. After years of movement through borders, checkpoints, waiting lines, holding areas and bus rides, the quiet pressed in around her like a wall. And in that stillness, the weight of everything caught up to her. She wept.

Not just for the family they had left behind, or the home they could never return to. She cried for what they had found, for the miracle of arrival. For the terrifying and beautiful act of beginning again.

For the first time in a long while, they weren't running anymore. She looked around the room, still in disbelief. So far from the place she was born. So far from the camps. It was all so overwhelming.

The Hansons opened their home with the generosity of people who understood they weren't just welcoming guests. They were receiving a family who had arrived with nothing but hope, a small child, and the quiet, aching of survival.

Their home was nestled among the trees with clean

walls, carpeted floors and working appliances. After years of straw mats and rationed water, it felt unreal. There were no dirt floors here. There were no communal fires used for heat, or shared latrines. They finally got to experience the luxury of clean linens, private rooms and a hot shower. All the things they didn't have, even before the war started.

Mrs. Hanson led them gently down a narrow hallway, speaking slowly in English. Mom and Dad didn't understand the words, but they didn't have to. Her tone carried kindness. She pointed to the kitchen, the bathroom, the bedrooms—each space humming with the soft whir of the heater through the vents and the quiet buzz of nightlights glowing in corners. There was a microwave, shiny and blinking. A washing machine with buttons that lit up. Faucets that spilled hot water on command. Mom stared at everything, her mind trying to catch up with her eyes. It was all new. All foreign. And in its quiet abundance, almost intimidating.

When they returned to their room after the tour, it was warm. One bed sat under the window, layered with thick blankets. Another bed waited against the opposite wall. The plush pillows had a softness Mom had never rested her head on before. She bowed slightly, offering the Hansons a quiet thank you with her eyes. Her smile was small, but full. Dad said nothing, he soaked it all in. He sat down on the bed and exhaled.

They were beyond tired. Jet lag curled in their limbs, heavy and slow. Without a word, they washed their hands and faces in warm water and laid down. The sheets were unfamiliar against their skin. They didn't even pull the blankets all the way up. They sank into the bed, together, safe, in a place that for the first time in a long time, didn't feel hostile.

They woke to the smell of something they couldn't recognize, filling the home. Dinner was ready. Mrs. Hanson called it a "classic American meal." A pot roast, tender and fragrant, sat at the center of the table. Its juices pooled at the bottom of the dish, soaking into thick slices of meat that fell apart at the touch of a fork. There was a salad, crisp and green, shiny with something called Italian dressing. Warm bread rolls, golden and soft, steamed as they were broken open.

Mom was full of amazement and curiosity. It smelled rich. Different. Lovely. She wasn't sure what to expect, but her stomach answered for her.

They sat together, Mom cradling Saeng in her lap, her small hands gripping the edge of the table. The Hansons gestured with smiles and wide eyes, pointing to plates and food. No one spoke the same language, but everyone tried.

Mr. Hanson asked slow, simple questions in English. Mom and Dad responded in Lao. There was laughter. There was confusion and joy in the absurdity of it all. No one really knew if they were answering each other correctly, but it didn't seem to matter. There was kindness in the room that filled the space where words couldn't reach.

That night became a memory Mom never forgot. It wasn't just their first meal in America. It was their first real taste of grace. They went to bed again with full stomachs and softened hearts. And for the first time in what felt like years, they weren't bracing for the next thing. They weren't preparing to leave. They weren't calculating what could go wrong.

They were in a stranger's home, in a foreign land, in a language they didn't speak. But they were welcome. Wanted. And that, too, felt like a kind of miracle.

The next morning, they woke to a world transformed. Mom pulled back the blinds and gasped, pressing her fingers to the cold glass. Outside, the city was wrapped in a soft white blanket. Snow. It coated the earth like a quiet miracle. Saeng stirred in her arms, and Mom lifted her to the window. Together, mother and daughter stared out at a landscape neither had ever known. Flakes drifting lazily from the sky, cloaking rooftops, trees, and roads in pure, silent white. It was the first snow they had ever seen. The first snow Saeng would ever touch.

The Hansons were already up, their faces bright with excitement at the morning's surprise. They gathered hand-me-down winter clothes as quickly as they could. There were jackets a little too big, scarves, wool gloves, and rubber boots. Layer by layer, they helped bundle Saeng against the cold, laughing softly at how strange it all felt.

Outside, their boots crunched against the snow-covered ground. Each step was tentative, filled with awe. The cold bit at their cheeks, but the wonder in Saeng's eyes warmed Mom and Dad's hearts. The little girl toddled through the powder, giggling as flakes landed on her lashes. Mom knelt beside her, scooping snow into her palm and marveling at its softness and fleeting form. After so many years of jungle paths, mud, and riverbanks, this was something they'd never expected.

That morning, with cold air filling their lungs and a new world laid out before them, something shifted. The years of uncertainty, the ache of leaving family behind, the trauma of camps and crossings—they didn't disappear. But they softened.

In those early days, Sundays grew into new traditions. Instead of incense or temple visits, there were pews, hymnals, and the steady rhythm of life in the Hanson household. Every week, Mom and Dad followed the Hansons to church, nestled quietly among strangers in a country still blooming into familiarity.

During the week, their days were full and busy. Mom and Dad attended English classes at the local community center, scribbling new words in notebooks, repeating phrases until their mouths felt strange. Language was both a bridge and a barrier, it offered hope, but also reminded them of how far they still had to go. While they studied, baby Saeng stayed at the church's daycare, surrounded by other children whose parents were also learning to find their footing on this new soil.

The government provided a modest refugee support stipend to the Hansons each month, enough to cover classes, childcare, and groceries. But the Hansons' generosity went far beyond what was required. They drove Mom and Dad across town in search of sticky rice and fish sauce, hunting down small international markets hidden in strip malls.

Sometimes they returned home triumphantly, clutching a small sack of glutinous rice like treasure. Mom still laughs remembering Mr. Hanson holding up a dusty bag of mung beans, asking, "Is this from Laos?" His voice was confident but always just a little off.

One Sunday, the Hansons arranged for Mom and Dad to meet other refugees. It was another family they assumed would share a language, a history, a home. But when the other family arrived, it became clear: they were Hmong, not Lao. Though both had fled the same war, crossed the same river, their dialects were entirely different.

The Hansons looked puzzled. "But... you're both from Laos. Why can't you understand each other?"

Mom and Dad smiled politely, unsure how to explain that being from the same country didn't mean they shared the same words. Laos was a patchwork of countless pieces, each with its own tongue.

As months passed and their English improved, the Hansons shared how they had come to sponsor Mom, Dad, and Saeng. It had happened months earlier, on an ordinary Sunday. At the close of the church service, the pastor stepped forward with an invitation. The congregation was asked to join a refugee sponsorship program with families who were living overseas needing help resettling in the U.S. They placed photographs on the altar of families in the refugee camp, holding signs with assigned numbers and names.

The Hansons wandered forward, just curious at first. But when they saw the photograph of Mom and Dad holding baby Saeng, a young couple with hopeful eyes, they knew. Something unspoken passed between Mr. and Mrs. Hanson. They would do it. They would bring this family to their home.

Mom was speechless hearing the story. She'd often wondered how they'd ended up with such kind, generous strangers. But it wasn't just by chance, it was grace.

They didn't stay long in the Hanson home. After just a few months, they moved into an old duplex a few streets away. It was nothing fancy—worn floors, drafty windows—but it was theirs. They shared the bottom unit, while another Lao refugee family lived upstairs. The creak of footsteps overhead became a comforting sound, a reminder they were not alone. That upstairs family became lifelong friends still to this day, another unexpected gift of resettlement.

In 1981, just a year after arriving, my brother Jay was born. He was the first Lao baby in our family that was born on American soil. A child of this new world. Mom remembers how proud she felt, how symbolic his birth was. He represented everything they had risked for: a future. A beginning. A name without borders.

Life in the refugee program was structured and

supportive. Each morning, the church shuttle arrived on schedule, carrying them from the duplex to their English classes. But the help they received went far beyond language lessons. The Hansons made sure Mom and Dad gained practical skills and opportunities to connect with others.

Mom enrolled in sewing classes, where her fingers, already nimble from years of mending and weaving in the camps, revealed a natural talent. Her teacher praised her eye for detail, her steady rhythm in stitching. This time, she got to learn how to make fun things. Like coasters and pot holders out of yarn. Crocheted winter hats and scarves. Meanwhile, Dad attended food service training at Edmonds Community College. He learned the ins and outs of working in a kitchen by reading tickets, handling equipment, and measuring portions. It wasn't glamorous, but it was a step forward. A foothold.

And that's what those early years were made of, footholds. Small victories. A kind smile by passerbys. The first time they answered the phone and understood the voice on the other end. The first class. The first snow. The first English word from Saeng's mouth.

Even with the Hansons' unwavering support, some days were hard. They missed Laos, and the family they'd left behind. They felt invisible at times, unsure how to ask for help beyond the Hansons. But they were determined to rebuild and become part of the new world they were in. One English word at a time. One stitch, one class, one prayer at a time.

But Mom and Dad had no idea what the true weight

of winter in Washington would be—not just the cold, but the way it swallowed sound, buried the familiar, pressed against the skin like an invisible hand. Snow was something they'd only recently started to witness. A novelty. A postcard image.

One early, bitter morning before sunrise, Mom pulled on her thin hand-me-down layers donated by the church, mismatched and a size too large, and laced up her secondhand boots. Overnight, snow had fallen heavy, blanketing sidewalks and burying any sign of the world beneath. Her breath escaped in clouds of smoke as she stepped outside of the duplex, the sky muted in that blue-gray calm only winter can bring. Each step left a soft print in the snow, only to vanish as the wind swept it away behind her.

She was headed to the bus stop, determined to make it to her sewing class. That class had become more than lessons, it was her routine in an unfamiliar world. A small patch of independence. A place where she could feel capable. Useful and American. She had come to rely on it, and especially on the bus that always arrived on time. Until that morning.

She waited. And waited. The cold gnawed at her slowly, like hunger—the kind of discomfort you think you can shake off if you just sit still, endure it a little longer.

Minutes bled into an hour. Then another. Buses passed, but none were hers. No one stopped. No one noticed the Lao woman sitting alone on a snow-laden bench, eyes searching the horizon, her face pale and stiff from cold. Her fingers stopped bending. Her toes no longer ached, they were numb. Still, she stayed. Because she was afraid. Not really of the cold, but of failing. Of missing class. Of disappointing the Hansons and not holding up her end of the life she'd promised to build here.

By the time she gave up, she rose, her body was numb and her thoughts slowed to a crawl. Cold wrapped around her like a second skin. She turned back toward the duplex, breath hitching as she forced her feet forward. The walk felt painful.

When she opened the door, Dad was already on his feet. One look at her and shock took over. Her lips were tinged with a frightening blue. Her hands shook violently, skin waxy.

Dad sprang into action. He pulled off her soaked coat and boots, hands trembling as he fumbled with the buttons. The pipes refused to deliver warm water fast enough, it was too cold. Without hesitation, he set pots on the stove, boiling water just enough to not burn her, rushing back and forth to the bathroom, pouring it into the tub like he was filling an ocean.

Steam clouded the room. Mom stepped in slowly, and the shock of warmth was unbearable. Her skin prickled violently, waking all at once. She cried, not just from the heat, but from the reality of it: she could have lost a piece of herself that morning if she stayed out longer.

She hadn't realized how close she'd come. That winter, snow became a new kind of enemy, silent and indifferent. In Laos, survival meant hiding from soldiers and avoiding landmines. In America, it meant learning how and when to go out during a snowstorm.

Mom laughs now when she tells the story, and says it was a foolish mistake. A lesson learned. That morning was a test of what it meant to start over in a place that didn't wait for you to catch up. It was humbling. It was unforgiving. She never missed another class since and she never let the snow get the best of her again.

They rarely talk about the day when the cold got the best of them. It felt like a flaw in their foundation, a sliver of vulnerability best left forgotten. But even in the most foreign places, their commitment remained. Mom and Dad were the one constant, steady presence through every trial. Having each other was the anchor that helped them endure anything.

That morning became a quiet vow between the memory of steam rising from a porcelain tub and the chill of snow in the air. A promise to look out for each other forever, no matter where they ended up. To make it through, always, together.

After months of uncertainty, where survival was measured in inches and instincts, life finally began to breathe in a steadier rhythm. The chaos softened just enough for a routine to take root.

Saeng was finally enrolled in school, a milestone monumental in its quietness. Her small body carried the invisible weight of two countries, two beginnings. By age five, she had endured more than many of her teachers ever had. And yet here she was, stepping into a classroom filled with foreign sounds and bright colors, clutching crayons and cautious optimism. The school was a world away from the humid, dusty corners of camp life or the cramped duplex where she now slept. But it was the beginning of something special.

Still, the transition was anything but gentle. There were days when Saeng had so much to adjust to, unable to explain the strange customs or the fast words she didn't yet understand. One moment, in particular, stands out—a common schoolyard inconvenience that grew into something much bigger. When Saeng came home scratching her head, Mom noticed the tiny bugs crawling in her roots—the dreaded head lice.

Having never encountered them before, Mom didn't know what they were, let alone how to treat them. They seemed endless, and no matter how hard she tried, she couldn't get them all out. Desperate and unsure, she did the only thing she could think of. Mom shaved Saeng's head.

For a little girl in a strange new world, it was more than a haircut. It was a mark of difference, a source of silent shame in a place where she already felt like she didn't belong. Saeng carried it quietly, as children of immigrants often do, balancing the innocence of childhood with the inherited grit of survival. She had no words for the complexity of it all, but she never forgot how it felt.

Around that same time, Mom was offered a chance, and a new door opened. It was her first job in America. With the Hansons' help, she began working at

McDonald's as a cook, a role both humbling and victorious. She wore her uniform proudly. Her English was broken, her steps careful, but she held her head high as she learned to compile ingredients for a burger, wrap them in waxy paper, slide them down the mini chute, and clock in with the same determination that had once carried her across the Mekong River. It was more than just a job, it was a declaration. They were still standing. Still moving forward.

To Saeng, it meant her mother was part of this new world. It meant Happy Meals and napkins printed with golden arches. The nostalgia of the first time she bit into a cheeseburger, the way the beef, pickles, cheese, and ketchup melted together in a taste she didn't yet have words for. It was just a burger, but to her, it was magic. A sweet, tangy bite of America. A small, joyful fragment of childhood she could finally call her own. Burgers remain a guilty pleasure, bringing back memories all these years later.

For Mom and Dad, that job was more than just a paycheck, it meant they could start living. Not merely to survive, but to participate. They could work, save, and contribute. Slowly, they could imagine a life no longer tethered to rely on the generosity of strangers, even as their gratitude to the Hansons remained unwavering.

That gratitude wove itself into everything they did. The Hansons had become more than sponsors, they were witnesses to their becoming and stewards of their dreams. In the hardest moments, the Hansons' kindness steadied the ground beneath my parents' feet. Their belief in second chances helped shape the world I would eventually be born into.

The church gave a gift that would create more independence for their daily lives: a used car. It was a simple, aging sedan that ran. They shared it with the Lao family upstairs, a reminder of how deeply their lives had become interwoven. That car represented progress—tiny, squeaky, and sputtering, but progress all the same.

In 1981, with a new baby in her arms and a life beginning to form around her, Mom sat down to write a letter. It was the first letter she had sent to Luang Namtha since their escape. She poured herself into every stroke of Lao script, the weight of years etched into each word. She told her mother they were safe now, that Saeng was in school, that Jay had been born in America. She missed them all dearly, and she explained how sorry she was for leaving without saying goodbye to her mother and siblings.

What she didn't say, what she couldn't say, was how much guilt still lingered. How often she saw her mother's face in her dreams. How much she ached for their safety too, how she missed the familiar scent of the village, the sound of wind rustling through coconut and banana trees—the rhythms of a life lost. Mom didn't want to make the letter more painful than it needed to be. She just wanted to let them know they were okay.

A year passed before they got a reply. The letter came in a weathered envelope, Lao script faint but unmistakable. Her sister's handwriting trembled with emotion. She wrote about how they had feared the worst, that Mom and Dad had perished, that they would never hear from them again. They hadn't known if either of them had survived.

Her sister wrote that when the letter finally reached them, it had been buried under a mountain of useless mail. They never expected to hear from Mom. When they found it, they wept with joy, passing it from hand to hand as though it were a precious treasure. At the end of the page, her sister asked for one thing: to thank the people who had helped Mom and Dad along the way. To thank the Hansons.

Meanwhile, Dad's friendship with his professor at Edmonds Community College became more than just about classes or career paths, it nudged open a door they didn't even know was possible.

The professor was a quiet man, in a kind and generous way. He'd noticed Dad's work ethic, his dedication to long hours with easy humility. He approached Dad with an unexpected opportunity. The professor's elderly aunt, who lived alone in Pensacola, Florida, needed help—someone to care for her and manage the household. He wondered if Dad might be willing to move his family down there. A fresh start, maybe. He offered to cover housing and to pay Mom a steady wage for cooking and cleaning. The man felt confident they would be great caretakers for his aunt.

It was an offer that made Dad stop and sit with it for a while. Saying yes would mean leaving behind everything they'd just begun to stitch together in

Washington: the small rituals of safety, the rhythm of familiar streets, the warmth of the Hansons' living room. It meant starting all over. Again.

At night, Mom and Dad talked in low voices after Saeng and Jay had gone to bed. They weighed what-ifs against maybes, uncertainties against hope. What would this mean for the kids? For their future? For the fragile sense of home they were trying to build from scratch?

By the spring of 1982, the decision was made. They packed again. It had become a familiar ritual, folding their lives into bags, trying not to leave too much behind. The Hansons stood with them on the curb the morning they left. Mr. Hanson placed a hand on Dad's shoulder and said, with quiet certainty, "Call us. Let us know you're safe."

Florida felt both foreign and familiar the moment they arrived. The air was heavy with humidity—similar to Laos, almost comforting. But everything else felt off-kilter. The community was different. The people were different. There were no familiar faces, no Lao voices coming from upstairs. They didn't know if there were any other Lao refugees there. In Washington, the church community had plenty. Here, they only had the flat sprawl of a southern town and a silence that settled in.

Mom took care of the professor's aunt with care and dignity by bathing her, feeding her, and keeping the house in perfect order. When she was done with her tasks, she took Saeng and Jay to the beach sometimes, watching them play and run across the sand. But the days began to feel stretched thin. The silence of the house was loud.

Mom's loneliness crept in slowly, like a shadow growing longer at the end of the day. There were no neighbors who spoke her language, no one to relate to and connect with.

One day, she picked up the phone and called Pom. Pom was from the same refugee camp, someone who remembered the nights under tarp roofs, the shared laughter over too-thin soup. Her voice, even through the phone line, brought some warmth. She told Mom about Colorado. About Denver. A place with mountains that felt strong and steady. A Lao community that gathered to attend the Buddhist temple and shared recipes, where her friends' kids called her "Auntie."

There was something in Pom's voice that softened the air. Something that made it feel, for just a moment, like home wasn't so far off.

Dad didn't need much convincing. Florida had worn him down, too. He said they had done their best there. That maybe, it was time to try again. He called the professor and explained they wanted to move on for more opportunities. The professor listened, then thanked him for everything. He agreed to hire someone new and told Dad he understood.

And just like that, the road curved again. Toward Colorado. Toward somewhere they'd never seen, but hoped they might belong. Their journey unfolding from one place to another, until they could find a permanent place to call home.

Saeng and Dad went on the road in their small brown Toyota Celica, driving from Florida to Colorado with their belongings. Meanwhile, Mom and Jay flew ahead, the plane cutting through the sky toward a new beginning where they would meet.

When they arrived in Colorado, they moved into an apartment complex where many refugees from the camp had settled. They were met with familiar voices, shared laughter, and the scent of Lao cooking, these small things began to mend the pieces of their scattered past.

Mom felt the loneliness fade as she and Dad found relief in securing a place to live. Reconnecting with old friends and rediscovering the community they'd missed, they stepped into their new life, carrying their past with quiet strength and embracing the future ahead.

After five long years of residency—years marked by sacrifice, hard work, and perseverance—Mom and Dad made a decision they had once only dared to dream about: pursuing U.S. citizenship.

For three months, they studied with quiet determination, poring over questions about American history, government, and civic responsibility. The material was challenging—not just because of the language barrier, but because of what it symbolized. Mom and Dad studied side by side, every answer memorized a step closer to something bigger: belonging, stability, and a voice in the place they now called home.

When they passed the exam, it wasn't just a legal

milestone; it was a moment of deep, overwhelming pride. In that instant, they were no longer just immigrants trying to survive in a foreign land. They were citizens, recognized and affirmed by the very country that had once felt so unfamiliar.

The natural simplicity of the ceremony belied its profound meaning. Standing in a room with others who had journeyed from all corners of the world, they raised their right hands and took the oath. It was more than a promise to uphold the Constitution, it was a declaration of belonging. They no longer had to live in the shadows, fearing their status or future. Mom and Dad could fully be a part of this country—openly, proudly, and without fear.

Walking out of that ceremony, heads held high, they carried with them the weight of everything that had brought them there: the perilous journeys, the lost loved ones, and the quiet strength it took to begin anew, time and time again. Citizenship was far more than a piece of paper, it was a new chapter finally written in their own name.

Yet, not everyone in Colorado's Lao community shared their optimism. Some criticized Mom and Dad, questioning why they had worked so hard to become American citizens. They saw it as a betrayal, a loss of connection to their Lao roots. But Mom and Dad never felt that way. They knew who they were and where they came from, and becoming citizens would never erase that. They stood firm in their belief that this was the right path, the ability to say "we're here to stay" was one of the best decisions they ever made for our family.

Since then, life unfolded with promise, each new door opening a little wider. Not long after settling in Colorado, Mom and Dad both found steady work cleaning the campus at a local university in Boulder. It wasn't glamorous, but it was reliable—a foundation on which they could build the future they had long dreamed of.

By 1986, I was their last-born child and the newest link in a chain stretching across continents and generations. Jay and I were the first-generation Lao-Americans in our family, our roots firmly planted in a homeland far away, while our branches reached toward an unfamiliar sky. The distance between where Mom and Dad had come from and where we were now seemed almost impossible to bridge, yet somehow, it was becoming our story.

It would be fourteen years after Mom and Dad's escape from Laos before the family could afford to return for a visit. In 1989, they brought with them not only the weight of survival and untold stories but also the three of us children—back home to the village where their own origins began.

I was just three years old, too young to hold those moments in my memory, but a reunion that was once an impossible dream had finally become real. Dad's family greeted Saeng like an old friend, while Jay and I were new faces in the fold—strangers embraced warmly by the widening circle of kin.

Mom recalls the flood of emotions that came with

that reunion: joy and relief, grief and pride, all tangled together. So many milestones had passed in their absence. So much had shifted beneath the surface of the land and the place they once called home.

Their journey had been long—marked by loss, perseverance, and hope—but now, with their own family gathered beside them, they could finally feel just how far they had come.

When we returned, our life in Colorado continued with a blend of change and cautious optimism. We lived among fellow Lao immigrants for a little while longer. Spending our days in that modest, low-income brick apartment complex, nestled in northwest Denver. The front doors of each unit were often left ajar, inviting neighbors to drift in and out freely. Kids ran up and down the narrow breezeways, their laughter echoing between walls. Elderly men and women sat in their living rooms, smoking cigarettes and exchanging warm greetings with those passing by. Lao families gathered to share meals and traditions. Forming a tight-knit community woven from shared history and resilience.

But Mom and Dad knew this cramped apartment was not meant to keep up with the five of us. They worked relentlessly, saving every hard-earned dollar from their cleaning jobs, determined to build a life that offered more space.

We finally outgrew that one-bedroom unit. After a couple more moves, Mom and Dad eventually managed to buy a ranch-style home in a quiet suburb about fifteen miles away. Finally, we had a place with a yard and separate bedrooms, where we could grow.

Leaving the apartment community marked a turning point, but it also stirred more whispers among some members of the Lao immigrant community. They said we had grown "too good" for them, accusing us of forgetting our roots once more. The words carried disappointment and maybe some fear that the bonds forged through shared struggle, might fray.

Mom, ever wise, reminded us never to feel ashamed of how far we had come. She taught us that in America, everyone has the power to choose their own path, and she was proud of the life we were building.

The suburban dream demanded sacrifices and tireless labor from Mom and Dad. Every paycheck was stretched thin, every hour on the clock a testament to their perseverance. Our house was wonderful, but inside of it, we grew up quite poor.

As a child, I overheard the complaints from some parents at school. They had opinions that immigrants were no good, other than to take American jobs. But it was never like those jobs were ones they were lining up for anyway. The hardworking hands of my parents, and others like them, weren't something to resent—they deserved respect.

I saw the sting of discrimination firsthand. One afternoon, standing beside Dad in line at the grocery store, I watched the cashier's disdain as he fumbled over a simple question about payment. She scoffed, rolled her eyes, and was completely rude, treating him like he was less than human just for misunderstanding. A surge of helpless fury burned inside me, wishing I could scream at her to see the dignity in my father's worn hands and the courage in his struggle.

"You don't have to be mean," I whispered. But Dad snapped as we left the store, "Be quiet. Don't do that. Don't say anything next time." I was confused how I let him down when I was only defending him. How could he expect me to respect people who treated him this way? But he was teaching me to keep my thoughts and feelings to myself, to survive in a world that wasn't always kind.

There were other moments etched in my memory, like the day Mom came home weighed down by a day's harshness. Her shoulders slumped, face worn thin. She locked herself in the upstairs bathroom, and I heard her muffled sobs. When I knocked, she brushed it off, telling me to do my homework. But later, I overheard her talking to Dad. Her shame and hurt were clear as she recounted how her boss had called her stupid for misunderstanding which conference room to clean. "So are you stupid or just don't know any English, which is it?" I thought about how cruel that was, to say that to someone who worked so hard.

Watching my parents face such disrespect was maddening. They worked harder than anyone I knew, yet were often overlooked, belittled, made invisible. And yet, they came home pretending to be fine, masking the wounds with their resilience.

Those moments uncovered hidden vulnerabilities in our family's strength. At the dinner table, their silence held heavy unspoken words, softened only by the warmth of a simple meal. It was strength and vulnerability wrapped tightly together, a reminder that no matter what, they kept moving forward.

As I grew, my frustration swelled. I wanted to fight for them, to stand against the unfairness they faced. But I was just a child—powerless in the face of ignorance. The world didn't see my parents as the heroes they were—the survivors, providers, and warriors who made impossible choices to build a safe home. They didn't know the displacement and fear, or the hurdles they jumped to get here.

Looking back, I wonder if it would have even mattered if they understood how they survived against all odds. Maybe it wouldn't have. But one thing is certain: my parents' journey is a testament to courage, dignity, and a strength many could never truly comprehend.

WHAT WE BROUGHT ACROSS THE RIVER

5 | Lao-American

There aren't many people who can say they had the perfect childhood. No matter where we came from, all of us carry pieces of our past that shape us in ways unseen.

I was born in the mid-1980s, planted in a small white suburb where the 1990s unfolded around me like a kaleidoscope of neon colors and pop culture. I came of age just as the new millennium was flickering on the horizon, a millennial navigating the cusp of change.

Back then, school days were marked by Lisa Frank folders bursting with neon colored characters, and the unmistakable thwack of velcro as Trapper Keepers peeled open. Brandy's first album filled the walls of my bedroom. TLC and Destiny's Child sang about girl power and heartbreak. Whitney Houston's pitch in "I Will Always Love You", broke your heart to pieces. And Boyz II Men were pleading on their knees for the women they love, in songs about feelings my young mind couldn't understand yet.

The soundtrack of that era included the Goo Goo Dolls, Third Eye Blind, and Blink 182. MTV was still a channel where you could actually watch music videos, rather than reality shows.

All the boys were tethered to their Nintendo and Sega Genesis consoles, eyes glued to pixelated worlds waiting for the new Sony PlayStation to arrive.

Pagers were all the craze and back then we used

house phones, memorizing phone numbers of friends we dialed often. I don't know how, but I still managed to remember our house number today. Flip phones became the coveted luxury, but only a few classmates had one by the time we graduated high school.

The approach of the year 2000 brought a buzz of Y2K panic, with widespread fears of technology shutting down. Of course all that stir was for nothing.

Social media was a concept unheard of in my childhood. I wouldn't join MySpace—the very first social media platform—until I was 17, in 2003.

It was a great era to grow up in, watching times change and technology evolve. I got to see us go from cassette tapes to CD's, VHS to DVD's, the transformation of TV's and computers from boxy frames to thin screens.

The moment I stepped into the halls of my school, I was like a ripple in the water, stirring everything around it. I marched in wearing jeans so long they had to be rolled up and folded at the ankles. I wore long sleeved shirts, even on the hottest of days, when Dad wouldn't let me show any skin at school. I tossed my ugly haircut around, watching the suburban kids pass by through my almond-shaped eyes. My wide, flat Lao nose—a gift from generations past—stood prominently on my face. My skin was fair, a black mole sat beneath my left eye, a faint dusting of a black peach fuzz traced a mustache across my upper lip. And around my neck, my Buddha necklace swung loosely like a small talisman.

But whatever confidence I had, no matter how small,

dwindled year after year under their questions and cruel treatment.

Even now, as an adult, I'm still taken aback by how often Asians aren't seen as minorities or people of color. It's usually those who've never lived it, who can't understand the sideways glances and the invisible lines drawn between you and them. Because as a kid walking those hallways, I felt the awkward tension everyday.

It started off mild. For starters, it would appear that I was not Asian enough for their standards. "Amber? Come on, what's your *real* name, huh?" they'd say, like Amber was just a costume I wore. They expected something foreign, something impossible to pronounce. "What was your name *before* it was Amber?" I'd go home and ask Mom, "Ma, what's my real name? Do I have a Lao name?" She'd look at me like I'd lost my mind. "What you talking about? It's Amber, Saeng pick it from a book at the hospital." The truth was, Saeng was the only sibling with a Lao name. And since Jay and I were born here, we had American names stamped on our natural birth certificates from the start.

They played with the letters of my last name, "What?! In-A-Thong?!" I had no idea what a thong was at that age, but their laughter told me it was something to be embarrassed of.

They asked, "So which one are you, are you Chinese or Japanese?" Like those were the only two I was allowed to choose from. I told them I was Lao, but they couldn't accept it. "What the hell is that?" a boy sneered, "Whatever, you're Chinese!" It was decided for me, as if I were too dumb to know where I came from. As if they knew more about my life than I did.

The torment escalated over time. One day, standing in line after recess, a boy spat in the back of my hair and high-fived his friend like it was a game. I felt his wet saliva go through my hair and land on my scalp. I asked for a bathroom pass, rushed to the sink, and submerged my head under running water until the cold sting made my head prickle. I was disgusted. I locked myself in the large handicapped stall at the end and sat on the floor for a long time, until my teacher came knocking. She asked me where I had been. I told her I was waiting for my hair to dry.

They would pull at the corners of their eyes and stick their tongues out at me to gawk at me, like I was sick. I didn't understand the punchline. Even if I had been from China, what was so funny about Chinese people anyway? Why would that be a bad thing?

The years continued with more inappropriate questions, "Why do you guys eat dogs?" or "How come you know how to speak English?" I'd tell them we eat chicken and pork like everyone else. I'd tell them I don't know why I know how to speak English, I've spoken it for as long as I could remember really. Always having to explain myself, always forced to prove I belonged there.

I wasn't American enough either. Sometimes when someone asked where I was from, instead of Laos, I'd say I was from Boulder, Colorado. That only made things worse. "Asian people don't come from Boulder!" they'd say, laughing like I had told a joke. Like the thought of someone who looked like me being born in an American city broke some invisible rule of theirs. Their minds couldn't stretch far enough for me.

I was surrounded by kids who had never needed to learn about the world beyond themselves. They didn't understand what it meant to be the child of immigrants, to live in the in between. And back then, I didn't have the language to explain it. I just had the feeling, the discomfort in my chest that settled in and stayed there.

I was the only Asian kid in my entire class—and just the second Asian kid in my entire grade in that neighborhood. As the years went on, I hardly smiled in school. I became serious and anxious. I was always uncomfortable and felt a little alienated. I didn't look or feel like any of the girls in my class. Most of them had shiny barrettes, neatly pressed polos or dresses, lunch boxes packed with snacks I didn't even recognize—fruit roll-ups, string cheese, Squeezeit brand juice bottles. I stared at their lunches with fascination. Dad paid for me to have school lunch, never forcing me to bring our unfamiliar foods to school. I gather he understood, in his own way.

I had to learn how to accept things. I'd be agreeable and walk around lucky enough to be allowed to exist in their presence. I started to become the mute girl who always sat near the back. The one who was nice enough, smart enough, polite enough. With the belief that if I could be enough in all the ways that mattered, they would stop noticing the parts of me that didn't.

When Mom and Dad took me to Lao community

events, that was my opportunity to be amongst fellow Lao-American children. It should have been a more fitting environment for me, but it wasn't. Because we were living in the suburbs, the Lao kids asked me, "Why do you talk so white?" squinting like they were trying to see through me, "Why do you act so white?"

At a party, a little girl in the community took a cup of ice, pulled the back of my shirt open and poured it down between my skin and the fabric. I was mortified. They thought my manners were influenced by my fancy suburb and wanted to chop me down to size, to remind me I was no better than anyone.

At another gathering, a group of Lao kids invited me to play hide-and-seek. I was thrilled they asked. I wanted so badly to fit in, to be wanted by them. We snuck off to an abandoned building nearby, broken and sagging with time, the kind of place we all knew we shouldn't have gone.

I found a hiding spot behind a wooden door that barely clung to its hinges. I crouched low, holding my breath, waiting to be found. But time kept stretching, and no one came.

A sick feeling sunk in, I worried the kids might have run off, back to the party without me. I tried to open the door. It wouldn't move. I shoved harder. Nothing. Panic hit fast. "Hey!" I yelled, pounding my fists against the wood. "Help! Somebody, please let me out!"

Behind me, the room was hollow and dark. My voice bounced back at me. And then I heard their laughs on the other side of the door.

"Come on," one of them whispered. "Let her out, we're gonna get in trouble."

They hadn't forgotten me. They had locked me in. Even in the Lao community, even among our own, my family's move to the suburbs was a mark against us. A quiet betrayal. No one could let go of the idea that we had left them behind, that we thought we were too good for the old neighborhood. We weren't. But it didn't matter. That was the story they chose to tell.

And like before, I learned how to carry it. How to shrink myself to make others more comfortable. How to shut up, even when I was screaming inside.

It was all so bleak. The kids at school. The kids in our Lao community. I never belonged to either. I felt like a weirdo that wasn't meant to exist—not meant to be walking those halls, sitting in those classrooms, or going to community events. Everywhere I went, it felt like I was too much and not enough all at once. Not here. Not there. Not American enough. Not really Lao.

That in-between space wasn't just confusing, it was lonely. A loneliness that stuck to my skin and followed me everywhere. I ruminated over stupid, pointless questions. What did the kids at school want from me? Did they want me to vanish? To go back to China, as they said? I didn't know anyone there. Did the Lao kids want me to convince my parents to move back to the old neighborhood, to give up the gains we'd made so I could prove something to them?

Those questions festered inside me for years, tucked away in the corners of my adolescent mind like unanswered letters. I didn't know what to do with any of it. I just knew I was tired. Tired of feeling split down the middle, tired of having to apologize for who I was.

I never wanted to be popular. I didn't want a spotlight or to be seen as special. I just wanted to be ordinary. To be a part of the crowd unnoticed and be left alone if not befriended. To be another carefree kid with a full lunchbox, another face in a classroom without being pointed at, talked about, or made into the punchline of someone's joke.

It didn't take long for me to begin closing up. I began to avoid the mirror. I didn't want to see myself. I was sticking out far too much for this neighborhood and not fitting in with the kids that had parents from the same country either. I didn't know how to decipher what was going on inside me, this invisible kind of little girl ache that made no sense and also made too much sense at the same time.

There was also a disconnect between my home life and the other kids at school. At school, I watched other kids' parents trade carpool duties and schedule weekend playdates with one another. I saw how their parents helped make extravagant school projects they brought to school, practiced spelling drills for quizzes the next day, and guided their kids like second nature. Their support came easily—effortless and expected.

I didn't know that kind of academic help. I brought ugly and cheap school projects to school on a poster board with whiteout and black marker. I was forced to display them right next to the fancy and polished projects kids brought with entire solar systems and paper mâché. I fumbled through homework assignments if I got stuck. It was always up to me to figure out.

One night, I sat at the kitchen table, frustrated and overwhelmed by an assignment I couldn't make sense of. Mom noticed the tension on my face and asked what was wrong. She walked over and peered at my notebook, her expression softening—but not with understanding. It was something closer to regret.

"Oh…" she said, the word heavy with quiet resignation. "You know me and Dad can't help you with that. That's why you better pay attention in school, Amber!"

She meant well. She always did. But I hadn't intended for her to see the gap between us, that the language of my schooling had never belonged to her. She had already given me everything she could. But when it came to academics, especially once it got complicated, I was on my own.

And despite the tired stereotype that "Asians are good at math," I was absolutely not. When I struggled, Mom told me to ask Dad. After all, math was supposed to be universal—two times two equals four, no matter what language you speak.

But boy did I quickly regret asking for help. "Why don't you get it? Take this number and count it this many times!" Dad would say, pointing at the page with growing irritation. His voice wasn't cruel, just sharp. Impatient. But to me, it cut deep. I wasn't just failing at math—I felt like I was disappointing him, like I was falling short of everything they came to this country for.

Mom and Dad expected the best from us. Education was everything. It was the only thing. It was a right that they were deprived of back home, one of the freedoms we left a country, a family, and a home for. Success in school was so much more than just about personal pride. Good grades weren't celebrated—they were the standard. And so, praise was rare.

When I visited other kids' homes, I noticed how their refrigerators were littered with colorful spelling tests, gold stars, and projects well done. Their fridges were a display of childhood achievements. Ours at home was just a blank, beige door. No report cards. No sign of what I do in school.

When I brought home a high score or a glowing report card, it never led to a pat on the back. It led to some strange lecture.

"Yeah, you have to do it," Mom would say flatly. "We have to do cleaning job, because we have no education. You have to be smart. Get better job."

In other words—duh. That's the point, Amber. That's why we're here. I learned early on that good grades weren't milestones. They were the bare minimum. So I stopped seeking praise and found another way to hold on to my wins. Every paper I aced, every project I was proud of, I folded them and tucked them into a box to stow beneath my bed. It became my secret scrapbook, a quiet place to store the proof that I was trying. That I was doing enough, even if no one said it out loud. In fact, much later in life, when I made the Dean's list for the first two years of college, I didn't even tell Mom and Dad.

But as time went on as a kid, I tried to make light of language struggles. I taught Mom how to rearrange English sentences that were backward when translated in Lao, laughing together at the difference in language. It helped to lighten things up between all of us.

For one, the sentence: *Going to my friend's house*, directly translated in our dialect of Lao would be—pai heun moo, which literally reads as: *Go house friend*. It was all backwards and it was no wonder my parents struggled with English grammar. So it was in the little moments like that, where I found some warmth and laughter with my parents amid the confusion.

My sister, brother, and I were the first of everything in our family. The first to have a life beyond the village fields, the first to hold diplomas or degrees, the first to speak English fluently and carry the weight of expectations that came with it. We were pioneers in a world our parents had only dreamed of. Yet, surrounded by classmates who didn't understand that kind of pressure.

At school, the other kids bragged about parents who chaperoned field trips or showed up to cheer at their soccer games. I stayed quiet. I had nothing to add. That kind of parental presence was a foreign concept to me. My world, the little suburban bubble I lived in, didn't understand my family or where we came from.

Most of my classmates didn't have parents who had lived through displacement, who had crossed rivers in the dark or fled from war. Their parents hadn't spent years haunted by the guilt of leaving people behind, or sacrificing safety for survival. They didn't live with the pressure of their parents deciding between sending money halfway across the world to their loved ones or buying the clothes you wanted for school. No, my classmates' stories were different—East Coast roots, Ivy League colleges, and established careers. Some of their moms even stayed home, fully available to their kids'—baking, helping with homework, attending every school play.

My parents didn't have that luxury. At home, I could hear Mom and Dad whispering behind closed doors, arguing in hushed tones about how much to send back home and who needed it most. Those tensions weren't explosive, but they lingered. They hovered above their heads at dinner. The guilt of having built a decent life here always collided with the obligation to those still struggling back there. Every dollar carried weight. Every decision felt like choosing between two worlds.

If something came in the mail that wasn't a regular bill, they brought it to me or my siblings to decipher. At first, I was too little to understand half of it, stumbling over insurance terms and formal language meant for adults. But we were their interpreters anyway, bridging a gap we never signed up for. And if someone came to the door—a solicitor, a stranger—we were the ones who answered, who spoke on their behalf, who explained.

We were the translators, the cultural buffers, the accidental adults in a world we barely understood ourselves.

At home I was referred to as "Ee-Lah," the last-born, the smallest. Dad never said it, but I knew he held a soft spot for me. Though he never said, I love you, never hugged me out of the blue, I felt cared for in other ways. The way he made my breakfast, the way he took me to every dentist appointment early, and turned the TV to *Barney* for me without needing to be asked.

I idolized him. He had this ability to say as little as possible and leave you thinking a whole lot. There was mystery in his tattoos—those faded blue marks on his knuckles and shoulder blades, symbols of a life he never spoke much about. I once asked him what they meant, and he just smiled, tapped one lightly, and said, "When I was a monk." That was it. A whole chapter of his life wrapped into five words.

But I imagined it often, my dad draped in saffron robes, shaved head, meditating on some dusty hilltop in Laos. A boy with none of this yet—not the janitor uniform, not the sore back, not the burden of providing for three children in a country that barely looked at him. Just a man who had once believed deeply in something sacred. Sometimes I wonder if he still did. If his journey here had drained that peace from him, or if he just kept it buried under his exhaustion.

As much as I idolized Dad, he had many layers to him. He was like a storm. Where he would move around without saying a word, which could put you at ease one moment, but scare the shit out of you in another. It was never his intention to be this way, but he was hard to read and challenging to connect with at times. A man of few words, there was clearly a lot going on in his mind, you'd rarely know what he was feeling or thinking unless it was frustration. Now that, you would know.

I often wondered why he wasn't like other dads, relaxed on a Saturday, tossing a ball with Jay in the yard. Instead, he carried a heavy weight of worry, caught in a never-ending cycle of work and exhaustion the entire time I was growing up.

Dad has always been a worrywart. I've inherited much of the same attributes. But even now, he frets over small things that often have simple solutions, and us kids grew up to make it our mission to reassure him again and again.

I suppose his years as a monk taught him the power of saying less and reflecting more, but incidentally that also meant he'd hold onto his feelings inside even if it meant an eruption might be brewing beneath the surface.

I mostly saw him smile in rare moments, like community gatherings at Lao weddings, Lao New Years celebrations, or baby blessings. When drinks flowed and laughter spilled, for a brief moment, the burden lifted from him. He became at ease again—free and lighthearted, a flicker of the man I knew who lived beneath the worry.

I remember sitting in those noisy rooms at Lao community gatherings that stretched late into the night, hours beyond what any child could handle. The air was always dense with laughter, cigarette smoke, and the sharp clatter of dominoes on floor mats. Cards shuffled in the background as Lao dads shouted playful threats over rounds of poker, sitting cross legged on the carpet.

The smell of fried rice and grilled meats lingered in the air, mixing with the pungent scent of Tiger Balm some auntie had rubbed on her temples.

Gambling had become an unspoken epidemic in our community. What started as a way to unwind often turned into something more damaging. A lot of men and women in our community suffered gambling addictions. I didn't understand the severity of it then. I only knew that I was the tired kid, curled up in the corner of someone's couch, begging to go home, rubbing sleep from my eyes while all the adults refused to leave.

When the Lao kids wouldn't play with me, sometimes I drifted off to sleep right there in the noise. My small frame disappeared into the cushions of a couch while the chaos danced around me. Eventually, Mom would tap Dad on the shoulder, her voice gentle but firm, and remind him it was time to go home. We'd slip out of the house with the laughter fading behind us, and I'd fall asleep again as soon as the car's engine rumbled softly along the road.

I always felt it though, the bump of the driveway beneath us when we pulled in. No matter how deep I had slept, my body knew that familiar jolt. I'd wake because I knew we were home, but I never opened my eyes. I waited. Then came the part I loved most as a kid.

Dad would turn off the engine, open the car door softly, and scoop me into his arms, careful not to wake me. I'd let my head fall against his shoulder, breathing in the scent of his laundry detergent and the faint traces of cigarette smoke left behind from the gambling rooms. He carried me in as if I were something fragile, tucking me into my bed with care. Maybe that's why I pretended I was asleep all those times in the car, I only got to witness this side of him when I was asleep and when his only duty was to keep me safe.

When I saw the exhaustion in his eyes, the weight of his unspoken worries, and the burdens he carried quietly, he still showed me that quiet kindness when he thought I wasn't looking. I wanted to make life better for him. Even for as little as I was, I wanted to fix it. I had developed a desire to lift away whatever the hell was dragging him down, to allow him to take a breath, and to let him feel like everything was going to be okay.

On the weekends when we did stay home, Mom would agree to wake from her nap to entertain me. She'd play games with me on lazy Saturday afternoons. When boredom crept through the windows and none of the neighborhood kids would play. Checkers was our favorite. I'd gotten the board game one birthday, bright red and black, with plastic pieces that made a satisfying snap when they jumped each other. "Oh, okay... I win!" Mom would clap her hands as if cheering herself on. Those games were ordinary and unremarkable to anyone else, but to me, they were tiny pockets of joy. They were reminders that childhood could feel normal, even when the world around us felt a little strange.

Mom continued to carry her own sorrows. Like Dad, she never said much about what was hard. When the day was done, the nights where I'd hear her crying behind closed doors continued—muffled, restrained, as if even her grief had to be a secret. Each time it happened, I had the same ritual. I'd tiptoe through the hallway and press my ear against the wooden door, my heart aching without understanding why. And then, minutes later, she'd emerge with her chin lifted, wiping her face clean, calling us to dinner with a voice that gave no hint of what had just passed. She wore her strength like a shield—always for us, never for herself. But I always knew.

There were moments when we'd hear devastating news from Laos. News when a cousin got sick, an uncle had passed, or a childhood friend from their village hadn't made it through another season. Those were the worst. Mom would sit on the edge of her bed, sometimes with a letter crumpled in her hands or a long-distance call still fresh in her ears. But even in grief, she kept going. Because she had to.

When she did express herself, it was to tell us what she didn't like, tell us what to do, or what we were doing wrong. She was raised with grit and accustomed to losing loved ones (dead or alive), so for as small as she was, she was a tough woman.

It was like neither of my parents felt they had the room to fall apart or be vulnerable. Not in front of us. And in retrospect I couldn't blame them. They had built something from nothing, a middle-class life that looked simple on the outside but had cost them a whole lot to get here. They wanted to preserve that. They never left room for emotions, when they had more pressing things to look after.

Still, whether we ignored it or not, there were so many feelings cooped up inside that house. A small, white and green ranch-style home, that was mostly brick, with three tall windows facing the street. I spent my summers climbing the giant cottonwood tree in the yard, never making it past the halfway point. The branches were always too far out of reach, taunting me.

Every year, those soft, white tufts of cotton would fall like snow, drifting through the air until they covered the grass like a gentle storm. I used to collect the tiny cotton balls thinking I could make one big enough, although I don't know what purpose it would be for. I was just a little naive girl without a clue, that while I made up stupid little tasks to do, Mom and Dad were counting dollars, planning meals, deciding which bills could wait another week.

Jay was the classic older brother who was more interested in teasing than in playing, unless it involved pretend wrestling or inventing games that somehow always ended with me getting the short end of the stick.

He once told me I was adopted, found in a dumpster behind 7-Eleven, and that the mole under my eye was the mark that proved it. He knew I hated that mole. No one else in the family had one, so of course he had to tease me about it. He said my mustache made me look like a boy. It was like he could read my mind and knew I secretly worried about that exact thing. I was maybe eight or nine, still too young to carry such shame, but old enough to understand what it meant to wish I didn't look the way I did.

I decided I had enough. Out of all the physical features I had, the little peach fuzz above my lip was about the only thing I could change. So while I couldn't change the way my eyes looked for the kids at school, or buy any name brand clothes, I could certainly shave my mustache. I rummaged through the bathroom cabinet, small hands reaching for one of Dad's disposable razors, holding it like a key to unlock my own version of normal. Mom caught me before I could do any damage. "Ee-Lah, what are you doing?" she asked, alarmed. "Can I shave my mustache?" I asked embarrassed, avoiding her eyes.

Her reaction was a mix of shock and confusion. She warned me that shaving it would make it grow back darker and thicker, trying to scare me out of the idea. "Oye, don't listen to what he say." she said, placing her hands on one of my shoulders. "You look fine, it's okay!" I didn't believe her, not fully—but I remember the way her voice wrapped around those words, trying to toughen me up from a world that would, eventually, make me question my self-esteem as a girl.

Jay and I were five years apart which is nothing now, but back then it felt like a large gap. He was in middle school when I was dragging a backpack half my size.

Unlike me, he was popular in school, good-looking in that effortlessly disheveled way, and always surrounded by kids who laughed loudly at his jokes. He was good at it, being the class clown, and knowing how to socialize. I suppose people were drawn to his carefree spirit, one that never worried about tomorrow, but more about enjoying right now. I noticed how he handled our Asian differences to white kids differently. He joked about us. "Hey, if you can't beat them, join them!" He'd say. If kids made a joke about Asian culture, he participated in it, even if it was demeaning and kept it going. I guess that was his own way of making himself fit in.

Mom was always more lenient with Jay. To this day, I'm still not sure why, but she never expected as much from him as she did from me and Saeng. I remember being irritated—having to shovel the snow, scrub bathrooms, vacuum our rooms—while Jay was rarely asked to lift a finger. He was spared from the household chores, spared from the endless list of expectations that clung to us girls.

Saeng, ten years older, existed in a different orbit altogether. In my early memories, she was already blossoming into womanhood. She was cool and composed, with sunglasses perched on her face and

New Kids on the Block playing from her Walkman. She'd sit in my backyard sandbox, analyzing her pores in her bedroom mirror while I still collected rocks and played pretend. She was calm and distant, like a constellation—close enough to admire, too far to ever touch.

She was studious, responsible, always doing the right thing. Eventually, she got a boyfriend who was another Lao kid, from a different town. Mom was thrilled. The community buzzed with whispers of marriage, already painting Saeng's future in broad, hopeful strokes. Jay once asked Mom if they were too young to be talking about marriage. "No," she said without blinking. "It's normal in Lao culture. Me and Dad were fifteen."

Saeng was always the example. The one we were expected to emulate. I was supposed to study like her, be like her, and live up to her standard. What most people didn't see, though, was that Saeng bore the brunt of everything. She had walked through the hardest chapters with Mom and Dad. She had lived through the leanest years, the first moves, and the rawest struggles before Jay and I ever entered the picture. All the unprocessed grief and hope they carried from Laos landed on her shoulders first. She didn't just set the bar, we watched her hold it up.

Even though Dad was mostly mute, he continued to keep himself busy around the house with tasks like fixing a leaky pipe or checking the oil in our family car. If Mom dreamed aloud about changing something—new floors, or a shower door that slid instead of clattered—Dad found a way to make it happen. But Mom would tease him for being cheap. "He never hire people to do, always do by himself!" she'd tell us. We all knew the truth though, it wasn't about pride for Dad, it was about making do.

When he couldn't get something to work, I stayed far away. But when he could get it to work, I wanted to be there to watch his face and soak in his energy, when he was proud and satisfied with what he'd done. Regardless, repairing things was his love language. You just had to know how to read it. He'd wordlessly leave my bike by the front door after he'd filled the tires and tightened my brakes. I'd ride off down the street feeling happy and loved.

Mom's love was folded into our stacks of clothes she left in the laundry basket. "Go get your clothes," she'd say in the middle of multi-tasking, smashing some Thai chili's in the pestle and mortar, "I don't have time, today I'm very busy!" My mouth would water when she'd smash those peppers, I anticipated she was preparing to make a papaya salad. Shreds of papaya that were green and crunchy, from not being ripe yet, fresh squeezed lime juice, and spicy peppers that made your lips swell from the heat. I'd remove my folded clothes from the laundry basket and sit in it while I waited for her to finish cooking, obnoxiously, pretending I was driving a car. I broke some of the plastic cages around the sides, which annoyed the hell out of her.

In the third grade she surprised me with a more proper Buddha necklace that was made of real gold—delicate and gleaming. It was much nicer than the plastic one I wore. She let me know she had saved for months to get it. "Everyone at the temple have to wear a good Buddha necklace," she said, placing it around my neck like it was a missing piece to my puzzle. I wore it proudly.

I had been out riding my bike, racing the daylight as the sun began to dip low behind the rooftops. When I got home, sweaty and carefree, she took one look at me and her face changed. "Where is your necklace?!" Her voice cracked, sharp with panic. I touched my chest, and my heart sank. It was gone.

The scolding came swiftly about how expensive it was, about how I needed to learn what it meant when someone gives you something so valuable. I felt like it was the end of the world, that I had lost something Mom worked so hard to buy for me. Jay and I searched the neighborhood, walking the sidewalks with flashlights as dusk fell over the block.

"Dude, I can't believe you lost it dummy. You better hope we find it." Jay warned.

My eyes suddenly widened, as if it might better my chances of seeing it on the ground. After what felt like forever, he spotted it in the street, glistening against the black tar like a dropped coin from the sky.

Even now, I still can't believe Mom trusted me with something so valuable. But maybe that was her way of showing me who she believed I could become, someone worthy of gold and of tradition.

We mostly did okay, for an immigrant-American family. I kept myself busy, helped out where I could. My summers in the backyard sandbox were short-lived. After just a few seasons of building castles and burying treasures, Mom reclaimed that patch of earth for something more practical: her herb garden. She said we needed it for vegetables. That it would save us money in the long run, season to season.

She planted everything: cilantro, Thai chilies, cherry tomatoes, cucumbers, sweet basil, and that stubborn mint that spread like wildfire through the soil, climbing into every corner like it owned the place.

Each spring, we crouched down in the dirt together, pulling weeds and digging through tangled roots. That garden became her refuge. Even now, long after those years have passed, she still tends to her plants the same way she tended to us—with patience, with grit, with the quiet belief that the things you nourish will grow.

On weekends, she'd season ground pork in a mixing bowl while I sat beside her, peeling egg roll wrappers. My fingers fumbled through the stack. I rolled lumpy rolls that came out loose and uneven, while hers were perfectly tight like they'd been made by a machine. She'd glance at mine and laugh, soft but pointed: "If you don't learn to cook, no one will marry you." I'd roll my eyes like it was nothing, but a part of me always worried she might be right. Beneath the joke was something earnest—an old-world truth she carried from Laos, one she believed still held weight here.

Sometimes we made *kalao pow* (gah-lao-pao). They were thick, fluffy dumplings stuffed with ground pork and chopped vegetables. They were warm and heavy in the hand, comforting in the way only food passed down through generations can be. The house would fill with steam and savory smells, the kitchen windows fogged with love.

One summer, Dad surprised me. He took me to the hardware store, just the two of us, and I watched him quietly select planks of wood, nails, and bolts. I didn't know what he was planning. But when we got home, he started building a swing set in our backyard—he looked at black and white pictures on the manual, not quite reading the instructions, but studying the images instead.

I watched him measure, saw, and hammer each piece with the focus of someone who didn't need words to show he cared. It was his way of speaking through labor, through craftsmanship, through something solid you could touch and feel. I swung on that swing set by myself for hours, day after day. It stood in our backyard for over a decade, weathering storms and seasons, a monument to his quiet devotion.

Years later, the wood began to splinter, the bolts rusted, and the beams cracked with age. We finally broke it down and carried it away piece by piece. But I never forgot what it meant—what he built for me, from scratch, in a language all his own.

In the earliest days, Dad and I shared the first half of

every day together, our own quiet stretch of time before Mom came home from her early shift and he left for his late one.

Each morning, I'd watch him steam sticky rice, the bamboo basket perched like a crown over the pot, steam unfurling into the kitchen with a fragrant cloud. I'd sit nearby, asking silly little kid questions while he flipped the bundle of rice onto a cloth and packed it into its round woven container, his motions practiced and precise. It was his small ritual, the one thing he made without fail. Sticky rice was his signature—humble, consistent, and quietly comforting. Even now, the scent of sticky rice brings me back, unlocking a thousand mornings all at once.

When Mom came home, I'd run to her with something to show—scraped knees, broken toys, or dramatic retellings of my day. "Jay ripped the nose off my teddy bear," she'd sigh, drop her work bag, grab a needle and thread, and sew the nose back on without skipping a beat. No lecture, no fuss. Just her silent way of fixing what was broken, of handling life with the same hands that would stir the pot of stew for dinner.

Mom and Dad passed each other like ships, each steering the household in their own direction, meeting only briefly in the middle. They gave so much of themselves just to keep the wheels turning. That rhythm became our foundation, an unspoken agreement through long days and tired eyes.

Weekends meant going to the Lao Buddhist temple. That was our sacred space, a tether to everything Mom and Dad had left behind. Mom lit up when I agreed to wear traditional Lao dresses, layered in thick patterns and gold trim that clung heavy on my frame. I hated the itchy fabric and the sweaty nude tights she insisted I wear underneath, but I wore them anyway.

The temple was Mom's place to breathe again, a place where she wasn't just another immigrant woman punching the clock. She was herself there: fluent, graceful, respected in a way she wasn't at her job.

There, we practiced *Tak Bat* (Tuck Baat), the sacred almsgiving ceremony. The monks sat in stillness, their robes a sea of saffron and gold. We knelt on the floor, inching forward on our knees with silver bowls filled with rice, fruit, or sweets. I remember how long those lines could feel, the slow ache building in my legs, trying not to squirm as the monks chanted blessings that rolled through the room like thunder underwater. Even now, those chants echo in my memory like a lullaby—melodic, ancient, and grounding.

There were other rituals, too. We gave offerings of money folded into origami flowers for ancestors I never knew, sandalwood smoke curling through the air, the sharp clink of metal bowls, the soft hush of people folding their hands in prayer. While the neighborhood kids were splashing at pools or riding roller coasters, I was offering sticky rice to monks and watching Mom pray for relatives I couldn't name, with stories I didn't fully understand.

That was home. That was us. Not flashy or thrilling, but steady. Rooted in something deeper than words. I didn't always love it then. But now I see the beauty in the culture, the discipline, the devotion, how our way of life needed to be.

I found comfort in our quiet life, in the predictability of home. In the way cooking with Mom or watching Dad make something work again, filled the space with something special.

Sometimes, Mom and Dad stumbled as they tried to navigate our lives. We weren't just learning how to adjust to a new country, we were also waiting for everyone to adjust to us.

Like when Dad dropped me off at school even though it was closed. I was only five, but for some reason, that memory stayed with me all these years. I wandered the empty playground alone until my teacher spotted me through a window and came outside. "Why are you here today?" she asked gently. I told her I was waiting for school to start.

As it turned out, a note had gone home earlier that week about the closure, but Dad never read school announcements. He didn't even go to parent-teacher conferences. She brought me inside and helped me call home. When Dad answered, he apologized and returned to retrieve me. Later that evening, he asked me to sit with him, help mark the school calendar by circling the days I didn't have to go. So I did. I was five.

I remember desperately wanting things I thought were "American." Like the sparkly jelly sandals all the girls were wearing at school. I begged Mom for a pair, and she did her best. We went to Payless Shoesource, and we found them. They were glittery, plastic, just like what everyone else wore—but one size too big. "So you can wear for long time" she said with pride. At first, I was thrilled. I paraded around the house, proud that I finally had the shoes that made me feel like I was one of the girls.

But when I wore them to school, I looked down under my desk and suddenly saw them differently. They were too big, too shiny, too noticeable. I curled my toes inside them, trying to keep my heels from slipping out. Still, when Mom picked me up that afternoon and asked, "Do you like them? Are you happy?" I nodded. I didn't want to hurt her feelings. She had tried. She always tried.

When I overheard one of the girls in my class was having a slumber party for her birthday. I came home that day and asked Mom, "Ma, if I get invited to sleep over, can I go?" She looked confused. "Huh? Why you want to sleep someone house? We have our own house!" Her voice held equal parts suspicion and disbelief. I went on to explain it's just what kids do, it's fun, it's normal, but she shook her head, unconvinced. "Eh-lah," she said, "we don't even know those people." To her, the idea was absurd. To me, it was another example of something I wanted so badly to participate in, to feel like I wasn't always standing on the outside looking in.

But even with those little gaps in understanding, we figured things out together. We learned how to adapt, how to look after one another, how to bridge the unfamiliar terrain between two worlds. We didn't always get it right, but we were trying.

And even though Jay teased me relentlessly, he looked out for me in his own way. When food was scarce, he showed me how to make sticky rice shaped like burritos. He'd flattened it in his hand, put a little dry shredded seaweed and a sprinkle of salt inside, rolled up tight. "It's good! Poor people food," he'd say with a grin. It was good. Sometimes we had to stretch what little we had, but we made the most of it. We had a few "poor people" go-tos. Mom would take sticky rice and flatten it into a circle, spread fermented bean paste on it and crisp it on a pan. I called it Lao pizza. Other times we ate MAMA noodles. An Asian version of America's cheap Top Ramen. We'd beef it up, crack an egg into the boiling broth and top it off with chopped cilantro, green onions and lime.

I often wondered what other families were eating in their homes. What did their dinner tables look like? Our family's opposite work schedules meant we never once sat down together to eat or share anything about our day. Mom would cook big portions, store them in the kitchen, and each of us would help ourselves whenever we were hungry.

I was thrilled when Mom let me go with a neighbor who had a little girl in my grade. Her parents took us to a Wendy's drive-thru after school to grab a meal. When her dad called out their usual order into the speaker, everyone turned to me to ask what I wanted. I didn't know what to say. Even if it was one of the biggest fast-food chains in America, I had never been to a Wendy's before. I'm sure not knowing what kind of food they served there must have looked a little odd to them.

Most of the time after school, my entertainment was TV. I didn't relate much to the shows everyone else talked about at school—*Full House*, *Saved by the Bell*, or anything with the polished homes, full of smiling families with heartfelt lessons. I watched them sometimes, but I didn't see myself in those stories. Afterall, what would I really have in common with little Michelle Tanner or the popular cheerleader, Kelly Kapowski?

There obviously weren't any shows about Moms and Dads studying for their citizenship. There wasn't anything on cable about parents fighting over how much money to send back home or where the kid was whining at her parents to go home from the gambling house. If there was a channel with a show where the kids were stretching their eyes to make fun of the little girl at recess, believe me, I would've watched it in a heartbeat.

My curiosity gravitated me more toward shows with black families. *Family Matters* made me laugh—especially Steve Urkel, with his suspenders and nasally voice. But underneath the silliness, there was something comforting about the Winslow family. The dad argued with his son, they forgave one another, teased their neighbor, but there was a lot of love. They even had an aunt who was a single mom and the kids in the home had conflicts with their friends and classmates that seemed far more real than other families on TV. But that show was based out of Chicago.

A few years later, my choice of shows were the *Fresh Prince of Bel-Air*, where Will Smith was sent by his mom to live with his Uncle Phil and his family. Many of these shows had non traditional family dynamics, beyond the cookie cutter ones. I watched *The Wayans Brothers* and *The Jamie Foxx Show*. They were everyday people and families, funny and flawed. And while they were stories that weren't like mine, they were my windows into a world where people of color were centered and celebrated.

I couldn't articulate why at the time, but something in me felt more interested in watching them. I didn't know how to name the absence of Asian families for me to watch back then. I just knew those shows gave me something that white sitcoms didn't: a sense of the in-between, a mix of struggle and strength, of not being the default but still taking up space anyway.

I watched Garcelle Beauvais on *The Jamie Foxx Show* in awe. Her beauty was regal and effortless, and I convinced myself she had almond-shaped eyes too, searching for a sliver of resemblance. Not because I thought I looked like her. She was stunning, glamorous, the kind of woman who'd never be mistaken for foreign in the way I was, but because she was a beautiful woman of color on screen, with her name in the credits and her face in the spotlight. I didn't know how much I needed those examples. They were glimpses of possibility.

Jay walked by and shook his head at me, "Why are you always watching black shows, weirdo?" he asked once, his tone teasing but curious. I never gave him a real answer. I didn't know how to say, it was because I felt more interested in watching these shows more than anything else on TV.

I will attest that Mom had Thai soap operas she rented on VHS, from the small Thai market in the next town over. Long, dramatic, slow-moving stories filled with family betrayal, love triangles, and suffering. I'd peek at the screen and roll my eyes at the actors falling apart because their parents arranged their marriages with people they didn't love, where they'd cry in slow motion. I didn't speak Thai, so most of it flew over my head anyway. But I'd ask Mom what was happening in them. She would sit transfixed, her eyes glistening as the stories unfolded, her mind pulled back to a culture and language that shaped her before I ever existed. I could never relate to those village stories, but I observed that was the only world she understood.

Take Your Child to Work Day at school was like a golden ticket, a way to skip school for the day, to see the world through our parents' eyes. I was just as eager as the other kids to spend the work day with my mom.

Before sunrise, Mom and I left the house in the dark. We arrived at the university while the campus was barely waking. The halls were long and silent, trailing behind every footstep. In one of the common areas, a couple of students lay curled up on couches, backpacks as pillows, jackets pulled over their heads.

"See how hard they study in college?" Mom said, nodding toward them. "You have to work hard, Ee-Lah."

I asked why they were sleeping there. "They have early exam," she replied. "It's okay, I vacuum around them. They still sleeping."

She said it like it was normal, like of course she worked while students slept. That morning, I followed her like a shadow. I watched as she scrubbed bathroom stalls, picked up stray gum wrappers and coffee cups, and pushed a mop down endless tile corridors. The scale of her work stretched beyond what I could take in. It was my first time being inside of a college university, it was such a big school.

There wasn't anything for me to do that day except observe. So I did. I watched her move with precision, her motions practiced and fast, like muscle memory honed by years of repetition. I saw how often people passed her by without acknowledging her, how invisible she became in that space and how used to it she was.

When lunchtime came, we ducked into her janitor's closet to eat. Although it was a big closet, it had no windows and made me claustrophobic with the scent of bleach and floor wax. We sat on overturned buckets. There was no table, our jackets were hung on a hook in the wall, there was a large faucet with a drain below that was meant for filling up the mop bucket. I leaned up against a large shelf full of cleaning products. Mom smiled as she unwrapped our food, like it was a picnic. So we sat and ate, sharing sticky rice and stew from the container she'd packed earlier that morning.

Somehow, that little closet, with its buzzing light and cold floor, I felt a warmth towards her. I recognized the familiar smell of cleaning solution, it was the same scent that came home with her in her clothes. It was such a small detail I made sense of, an explanation as to where the smell came from, when I hugged her each time she came home.

Later, when I got fidgety and tired, she took her jacket off the hook, folded it neatly, and laid it on the cold concrete. "Lie down, Ee-Lah. I have one more room to finish. Be good and wait here." I did as she asked, but anxiety crept in. What if someone opened the door? What if they saw me lying there, a kid hiding in the janitor's closet of her mother's job? I worried about getting in trouble just imagining it.

Somehow, I drifted off anyway because she was gone for quite some time. But when she came back, she was holding a crinkled bag of chips—purchased from a vending machine with quarters she must've grabbed from her jacket when I wasn't looking. She handed it to me with a small smile, and just like that, I felt relieved she returned. That simple gesture meant everything.

The next day at school, our first task was to go up to the chalk board and write down our parents' job profession, so all the kids can see the variety of careers we got to shadow for the day. The list on the board piled up: dental hygienist, accountant, broker, and florist. I was next in line, I grabbed the piece of chalk and wrote it, I wrote it as fast as I could and put the chalk down. I nearly ran back to my seat, as if I was running from what I wrote down.

By the time everyone sat down to look at the list in its entirety, someone said it, "What's a Custodian?" And then another voice, "That's what Mr. Moody does!", said a girl referencing our own school janitor. "What? Who's parent is a JANITOR?!" The class laughed in unison. I didn't say a single word. I sat there mortified.

Once the teacher calmed the classroom down, the kids buzzed with stories about their day. They beamed as they described their parents' offices full of candy jars, computer games, catered lunches, and conference rooms that became playgrounds for a day. I just wanted the school day to be over. I didn't want to talk about the janitor's closet. And while I'd proudly tell people what my parents used to do today and how they served the state university for 23 years, as a child, it was completely different. It was hard to be proud of it. I didn't have much sense then and I couldn't help but feel embarrassed to say what my Mom and Dad did for a living.

Little did I know, that day had changed something in me. It doesn't have to come in grand displays or company swag. Sometimes, it's in the early mornings and vending machine chips. In the way a mother lays down her jacket so her child can rest, even for just a moment. That being a provider can be shown in many different ways.

I was still understanding the true shape of sacrifice and a way of life lived in service to others, even when no one is watching.

Those moments at school stretched through my earliest days—brief, fleeting, and painfully raw—as I struggled to be proud of who we were, to feel comfortable in my own skin, and to understand why the other kids didn't want me around. I was desperate to find anyone who would just be okay with me.

When a big event came up, the ice cream social, the whole school buzzed about it all week. In art class, we spent days cutting construction paper, gluing glitter onto posters, and coloring decorations for the gym. The excitement hummed through the hallways like static electricity.

There would be dancing, raffle prizes, carnival games, and a bake sale lined with homemade sweets. Brownies and cupcakes were donated by parents to raise money for the music program. I overheard one girl say her mom was bringing an extra batch for everyone to taste for free. That tiny detail excited me. For most kids, it was a simple kind of joy, a school day that felt like a holiday.

But that excitement vanished fast. During recess, I stood near the edge of the playground when one of the boys approached. His shoulders were tight, his lips twitching like he was trying not to grin. "Hey," he said, "my friend wants to ask you to the ice cream social." Behind him, a few other boys formed a loose circle, watching like they were waiting for a punchline. One of them pushed the boy toward me, laughing as if I were some contagious disease. I didn't need anyone to spell it out. The joke was written all over their faces.

My stomach flipped. My heart pounded loud in my ears. That poor boy clearly wanted nothing to do with me and looked like he'd lost some kind of dare. But it didn't stop the humiliation from blooming across my face. The heat climbed up my neck as their laughter spilled out. I turned away, feeling like something rotten was growing inside of me.

I asked if I could visit the nurse, saying I didn't feel well. It wasn't a total lie, but what I was feeling was shame rather than sickness. The nurse gave me that soft, knowing look adults do when they suspect there's more going on. She gently asked if I was sure I didn't want to stay for the event later. Then she asked if my mom was bringing anything for the bake sale.

That question landed like a slap. Of course she hadn't. She never did. Not because she didn't care, but because she didn't have the time, the resources, or the context to. We didn't bake for school fundraisers. We were barely keeping our heads above water.

I missed the ice cream social. I walked home that afternoon with the weight of it all pressing heavily on my shoulders. I hated the way I looked. I remember staring at my reflection in the mirror—my too-big Payless shoes, my mismatched clothes, my eyes, my flat nose, the mole and faint mustache on my face. I wished I could trade it all for something that made sense to the other kids.

Afterwards, everyone talked about the ice cream social for the rest of the week. Gleaming about who won prizes, who danced with who, who brought the best brownies. I pretended not to care, but inside, I kept circling back to that moment, the moment when I saw them laughing at me, as if my very existence was a joke.

I never talked back to the kids who mocked me. That wasn't how I was raised. I swallowed it all. I carried it. Let it build inside. In the days that followed, I lay on my bed without a sound, watching the ceiling fan spin, pretending it could blow away my dumb feelings. My backpack sat untouched in the corner.

I didn't tell Mom what happened. I never told my parents each time it happened. What would they do? What could they do? I worried Dad might tell me to keep my mouth shut at school, like after that incident at the grocery store. Or that Mom would just tell me not to care. I didn't think they'd understand it the way I felt it. To them, this was just part of being a kid. And maybe, in a way, they weren't wrong.

Still, it felt so unfair—to feel like I didn't belong before I'd even had a chance to try.

I couldn't ask them to fight this invisible battle too. I never wanted to bother them when they were working so hard just to give us a home and a hot meal. It was probably small in comparison to the troubles on their mind. So I watched more TV, gravitated toward the characters who were bold and funny, who made space for themselves even when the world tried to shrink them. Maybe I was hoping, somehow, that I could learn to do the same one day.

One day, while lining up for a school field trip, I caught a glimpse of the only other Asian kid in my grade. It was a boy I didn't know well, from another classroom. We locked eyes for a second before both looking away. I thought about him that night, lying in bed. Did he feel it too? The not-belonging, the ache of being seen but not understood. Maybe in some house not far from mine, he was wondering the same thing about me. The thought gave me a small, strange comfort. Someone else like me.

That memory of the other Asian boy in my grade, that brief glance we shared during the field trip line, stayed with me for years. We never spoke. Not once. I never learned his name. But in that single glance, something passed between us. Recognition, maybe. A kind of understanding that I'd been starved for. It was one of the only times I felt seen by someone who didn't require an explanation.

We never became friends. Maybe we both thought one misstep would give them even more reason to laugh at us. But sometimes I imagined a different version of our story, one where we sat next to each other maybe in school, shared snacks from our moms' kitchens, and talked about how weird all this shit was. How it felt to be asked questions you didn't have the answers to.

Sometimes I'd wonder if it would be easier to go through school with a different last name. Something easy to pronounce, like Smith. A name called out in class that would not be followed by a pause and then a

"What kind of name is that?" Scenarios where I'd have to explain Laos all over again. I wanted to wear jeans that fit right, maybe even join the Girl Scouts like the other girls did.

I don't know why I cared so much about being part of the crowd. I guess I'd watch girls giggle together and classmates group up to play at recess as I would sit there embarrassed looking at my hands like a dummy or walking alone. As if it was painfully obvious I had nowhere to go or be. I was desperate to be understood. To be able to explain why my parents never came to school events, why my clothes looked a little off, or why I couldn't go to girl's sleepovers.

I carried on politely, always trying to follow the rules, always hoping someone might ask me to play at recess or sit with me. But the truth was, I was invisible to most of them and when I was seen, it was never for any nice reason. It's a strange kind of awkwardness, that subtle and unspoken isolation.

Some of my childhood offered brief pockets of relief—moments where I could breathe a little easier, especially when I found a friend or two who wanted to know me. Like with Tory. I gravitated toward the occasional person who listened without judgment, who seemed genuinely curious about who I was beneath the surface.

Living between languages wasn't just about words, it was about identity. I spent my childhood performing a balancing act, trying to fit into a world that didn't always see me while honoring a home that never asked me to be anything but quiet.

At home, silence was survival. Out in the world, expression was freedom. I craved both, but they didn't coexist easily. Any time I wanted to open up about what I was feeling, I didn't know how—or worse, I learned speaking up would somehow betray the manners my parents taught us.

So I swallowed my questions, ignored my needs, and became good at keeping things inside. There was no space for emotional vulnerability. I walked a tightrope between who I was supposed to be and who I might have been if I'd felt safe enough to just feel.

This would cost me greatly when I had one particularly dark incident in my childhood, at the hands of those who were outside the walls of our home. For a brief, but traumatic time, my desire to be befriended and liked caused me to trust a couple of older kids who sought to take advantage of my trust in ways that cost me my innocence. But I felt paralyzed by my upbringing of silence, repressed my feelings, and paid dearly for many years to come. This would be something that resurfaced later in my life, something I'm still trying to resolve today. A chapter I don't know when I will be fully ready to share.

My parents did the best they could with what they knew. But they couldn't protect me from what I was experiencing outside of our home. It took years to understand that their resilience didn't mean they were untouched by pain. It meant they carried it without ever letting it stop them from taking care of their responsibilities. And I guess I tried to learn how to be the same.

But I wonder who we all might have become if healing had been a part of our vocabulary. If therapy had been seen not as a weakness but as a gift. If we had been taught that feeling things is its own form of strength. Maybe we could have shared more, carried less alone, talked about things, and loved more freely. Maybe keeping our mouths shut wouldn't have had to be our armor. Or maybe that's very American of me to say, because Lao people don't really think that way.

Incidentally, with the perspective of adulthood, I understand how much of it took courage. Their refusal to burden us with their feelings, was their own way of showing love. They gave us the chance to live a fuller life they could barely imagine, even if that life came with questions they couldn't answer.

That tension between silence and speech, between survival and selfhood—is one I carried with me for a long time. It's the inheritance of many children born in-between. But it's also where my own story began.

The pressure of all the unspoken things inside me grew big enough to where I eventually needed somewhere to put it. So I turned to writing. Writing became the one place I could be completely honest. I wasn't filtered or careful, I was just me. In the pages of my journal, tucked under my bed, I found a way to say what I couldn't say out loud. It was clumsy, but it was mine. And it was the first time I understood that my voice had value by letting it all out, even if no one else could hear it yet.

My parents continued on working tirelessly, the weight of responsibility never loosening its grip on them. Their love for us was steady and silent, woven into all the things they'd do for us without saying a word.

It brings me some resolve to understand their silence as its own kind of language. A dialect shaped by survival—by war, by fear, by having to flee everything they once knew. They couldn't afford to be led by emotion back then. If they had been, they may never have made it out of Laos at all.

Still, that nagging tug-of-war inside me festered. How could I be proud of being Lao, yet still be American enough for the world around me to let me in?

So while other kids were discovering hobbies, crushes, and who they wanted to be when they grew up, I was tangled in these dumb questions I didn't know how to ask: Who am I supposed to be? And what if there's no place where both parts of me fit?

I wanted to stop feeling like I had to choose between Lao and American, between fitting in and holding on, between who I was and who I wanted to become.

I suppose over time my defense mechanism was to become fluent in avoidance. I began to distance myself from my culture—not all at once, but slowly, almost imperceptibly. I stopped saying where we were from. I minimized the parts of me that made people raise their eyebrows or mispronounce something. It was as if being Lao was inconvenient at that point, something that got in the way of being accepted. So, I did what I thought I had to: I split myself in two.

I started to agree when kids complained about their parents grounding them or not increasing their allowance, even though I had no idea what that even meant. I mimicked their complaints to blend in, pretending I had the same experiences. But the truth was, I had never been grounded. I had never even heard the word 'allowance' used in our house. Like what the hell is that all about? Do kids really get money from their parents to do chores to teach them responsibility? In our house, it was our duty to help our parents all the time, without expecting a thing in return.

We washed dishes, shoveled the snow, massaged our parents' backs, that's what we were supposed to do. If an allowance was what these kids were complaining about, they wouldn't like the way things were run in our household.

And since I wasn't allowed to show skin, I started wearing short sleeved shirts to look a little more normal. I'd wear it underneath my sweater so my Dad wouldn't see when I'd walk out the door. But as soon as I'd get to school, I'd take my sweater off.

When I got home, I would put my sweater back on. I'd slip back into the other part of me—surrounded by our language, our food, our way of life. I'd kick off my shoes at the entryway and devour whatever spicy Lao dish was on the table. Carefully changing the way I spoke and carried myself around Mom and Dad.

The shift between those two selves became

automatic, something I didn't even have to think about. Like switching between languages, or changing clothes. A coping skill I didn't know I was mastering.

I kept both worlds neatly separated. One never spilled into the other. I knew which version of me was safe for each space, and I was careful about how I spoke, how I dressed, even how I laughed. Everything mattered, even the smallest things. And just like that, I was becoming my Dad, worried about every little thing.

I never liked inviting anyone over to our house. I couldn't bear the thought of what they might say or worse, what they might think and never say out loud. As soon as you walked into our house, there was no hiding who we were. At the entryway, our shoes were taken off and piled by the door. No one ever wore them past the threshold. A large photo of the Buddha hung in our living room, watching over everything. Nearby, a tall glass display case stood like a silent guardian, filled with golden statues and offering bowls—a revered shrine.

My parents sort of became pack rats over the years, so our house was cluttered. I wouldn't go as far as to say they were hoarders, but they accumulated and kept mismatched household items they collected from their cleaning jobs. We even used napkins and toilet paper they brought home from their work. We had too many mugs, too many pots, mismatched chairs in our living spaces, and the most random decor. I guess after experiencing so much loss, my parents had developed this incessant need to hold on to things—even items we didn't really need—because they were so used to not having very much.

In the backyard, my mom had her outdoor kitchen. It was set up with burners that ran on a propane tank, and old pots stained with spices that told their own stories. It's where she cooked the dishes that smelled like home: ingredients with fermented shrimp paste, pungent curries, and grilled meats that clung to your clothes long after you ate.

Eventually, Saeng helped build her a proper storage shed for cooking outside instead of the back deck. Even today, Mom still prepares meals out there in the backyard. That space became her domain, the place where she worked her magic. But back then, I knew it made us different.

I didn't want any of the kids in our school to see it. I worried they'd wrinkle their noses at the smells, see all the random things my parents kept, or ask questions I couldn't answer without feeling shame. I wasn't equipped to explain without turning red, without feeling like I had something to apologize for.

When someone asked to hang out after school, I'd suggest we go to their house. I always had a reason why mine wasn't an option. I told myself it was easier that way. After what I had already experienced, I stopped giving people the chance to show me any different. I assumed they wouldn't understand, so I made sure they never got close enough to try.

When Mom and Dad began working the same shift, Dad became a maintenance man, repairing things around the campus. I was relieved he could work days with her and not have to do such a late shift. That neither of them had to take turns with responsibilities at home, like passing a baton in a relay.

But as time passed, the weight of raising three growing kids pressed harder on our family. Expenses crept up with every new school year, every size increase in shoes, every unexpected need. Eventually, Mom and Dad had no choice but to take on second jobs. After their day shifts, they'd stop home for a quick bite with barely enough time to rest their feet before rushing back out for work again. In the evenings, they worked as janitors at a nearby daycare. When they needed help, they started bringing me along.

The daycare at night was a hollow shell of its daytime self. The noise and laughter that usually filled the rooms were replaced with silence, eerie shadows lurking in every corner. Toys sat abandoned, gathering dust. The scent of glue lingered on the tables like a ghost. Under the dull flicker of overhead lights, I moved slowly, afraid to make a sound and too aware to be carefree.

Mom and Dad handed me small tasks as soon as we arrived. I emptied tiny trash cans, wiped down smudged tables, picked up crayons and snack wrappers scattered on the floor. They handled the heavy work—mopping floors, cleaning bathrooms, vacuuming every room. Sometimes, when I finished my chores, I'd try to focus on my math homework. But it was hard to think straight under those buzzing fluorescent lights, with mop buckets clattering down the hall.

There was a small gym inside the daycare—a space

where, by day, children flipped on balance beams and leapt into pits filled with soft foam blocks. I ached to jump in just once, to feel lightness. But Mom said no. "We can't make mess," she warned. "No one can know you here." I wasn't there to play. I was there to help. I was there to work.

On nights they didn't bring me, I warmed my own dinner. I'd lift the red plastic basket from the kitchen counter, microwave whatever Mom left in the pot, and eat alone in front of the TV until they returned around nine.

Those nights were uneventful, but never peaceful. Something heavy settled in my chest during those hours—something unspoken, vast, and aching. I didn't resent them. I couldn't. But I resented the unfairness of it all. Why did we have to live this way? Why did I have to help my parents at their night jobs when I was just a kid? Why couldn't we be like everyone else and sit down for dinner together, laugh, talk, be a family in the ways other kids were? But I felt too guilty to complain. Too guilty to question.

Mom and Dad tried to hide their weariness, but I saw it anyway. It was evident in the slump of their shoulders, the way their bodies seemed to shrink with each passing year. On weekends, I'd perform Thai massage to get the knots out of Mom's back. She had tight muscles from years of bending, lifting, and scrubbing. She carried the weight of her job literally, wearing vacuums over her shoulder like heavy backpacks, dragging machines through long, silent corridors.

She taught me how to perfect my massage technique. "Use your feet," she said, patient but firm. I'd step carefully, walking gently across her back. I'd grip the wall for balance trying not to slip on the Tiger Balm slathered on her skin. It was a kind of Lao and Thai massage, a tradition passed down to me at a young age. As she lay face down, I imagined myself crossing a bridge over hot lava, a story I needed to imagine because stepping on her back was boring and took forever. Her eyes stayed closed, trying to catch some relief. She never said much, she took those moments to take pause and let go for a little while.

Those knots never disappeared, no matter how hard I tried. They became part of her, like the lines on her hands or the tired weight in her voice. Sometimes I did the same for Dad until I grew bigger, heavier, and the pressure became too much for his worn back.

Watching them, I felt a love that hurt. A love that ached and filled my chest with both gratitude and helplessness. They worked so hard, so constantly, to give us everything they could. And I wished so badly that their sacrifices didn't have to be so physical, so consuming. I wished there had been more time for laughter, more ease, more joy.

But this was the life they carried for us. A love that spoke in long hours and aching backs, in hot food warmed on the stove and shoes left at the door.

It was around that time I met Melanie. She lived just a couple blocks away, and every morning we rode our bikes to school side by side, baskets dangling from our handlebars, wind in our hair. Her parents were divorced, something not many kids we knew talked openly about yet. For the first time, I had someone who truly felt like a friend.

Melanie wasn't a popular kid. She had big glasses, curly brown hair, and was nervous in crowds. But with me, she was open and endlessly curious. We clung to each other from the moment we met. We were different from everyone else, perfect for each other.

She asked me things no one else ever had. About our food. About the temple. About how to say things in Lao. She was fascinated, but not in a weird, performative way. She genuinely wanted to understand. When she finally came over to my house, she thought our house was cool and different. That meant more to me than she probably realized.

Melanie lived with her dad and her younger brother Benny. Their mom had moved back to the East Coast after the divorce, and Melanie missed her terribly. She confided in me, told me how lonely it felt to be the only girl in a house full of boys. Her parents said the decision was for stability—to keep her in the same school, to preserve some sense of normal—but I could tell it never quite felt normal for her. Just like growing up Lao in an American suburb didn't feel normal for me.

We didn't share the same kind of hurt, but we both knew what it felt like to carry something invisible. Every August, we'd race our bikes to school to check the new class lists taped to the glass windows. I held my breath every year, hoping we'd be in the same classroom. If we weren't, I'd feel a small pit of dread open in my stomach. But it never lasted.

Despite whatever class we landed in, we always met at our usual corner—halfway between her house and mine—and went to school the rest of the way together. For those twenty-five minutes each morning, everything felt just right. We belonged.

Mom and Dad gave a lot so I could have even the smallest joys. When I begged to join the basketball team, they scraped together just enough for one season. One fleeting season for shoes, the uniform, late-night rides home with teammates. It wasn't much, but to me, it felt like everything. For a little while, I got to feel like any other kid. Part of something normal. I didn't even know anyone on the team; I guess I took the leap to force myself out of my comfort zone, to try to make a couple more friends.

My sister and her boyfriend made it to one of my games. They sat on the gym bleachers and cheered when I ran out with my team. After the game, Saeng approached me. "You have to be more aggressive, Amber!" That was just like her—tough, no-nonsense. Saeng was the survivor of the refugee camp; I was the soft one, born here.

Mom and Dad never made it to a game. Their time belonged to long hours and second jobs, to the invisible labor that kept our family afloat. I never brought it up. I never asked why or made them feel bad. That kind of disappointment felt like a luxury, something only spoiled kids could afford. Honestly, I was just relieved to be doing something else with my time. It gave me a little break from helping Mom and Dad clean the daycare at night.

Game after game, I watched the other parents waving handmade signs, shouting encouragement, snapping photos. I'd glance up and imagine my parents there too, even if only for a moment, just so I could feel alright about it.

It wasn't fair. They worked too hard to watch me play a sport I wasn't even good at. Truthfully, I barely knew what to do with the ball once I had it. I didn't belong there. But I still wanted to try.

After that season, I turned toward the things that didn't cost money. Choir. Drama. School musicals. Things that only asked for time and a little heart. I discovered something in make believe—a kind of freedom, playing a role to be someone else. On stage, I could become someone brave, someone beautiful, someone who belonged in the spotlight.

Melanie played clarinet in the school band, and I sang my way through the years in a group of Sopranos. Our paths sometimes crossed in performances, but music became my own private escape.

The theater became a second home. It was where I didn't have to be so conflicted about how I was supposed to act around people. A world where if I played someone else I could be anything, say anything, express anything the character was feeling.

I remember my first role in William Shakespeare's play, *A Midsummer Night's Dream*. The language was so confusing, but I spent many nights at home practicing the script before bed. I also played a peasant in the school musical *Kiss Me Kate*, where I sang with a group of girls as I swept the floors with a fake stage broom in formation. And for a brief moment, under the bright lights, I was someone worth noticing for a different reason than before.

When the curtain closed and applause filled the room, my classmates would rush into their families' arms, wrapped in hugs, their arms full of flowers and folded-up programs, snapping photos. I'd gather my things as quickly as I could, slip out the back doors, unlock my bike, and pedal home through the dark while Mom and Dad were at their second job.

The air was cool and sharp against my face. The road was dark, and I kept a steady pace, moving from one pool of light to the next, under the street lamps. And in that journey, I tried to carry the magic of the stage with me for as long as I could.

I watched the world change one flickering screen at a time. First, those clunky beige Macintosh computers where I played *The Oregon Trail*, solving math problems in pixelated meadows, my wagon breaking down every other mile. Then came those candy-colored Apple desktops that were neon green, electric blue, translucent and glowing like something out of the future. It was an exciting time. Sitting in the school library, fingers hovering over the keyboard, I felt like I was on the edge of something bigger.

When the internet arrived, it was like the universe

moved at lightning speed. That screeching dial-up sound that was clumsy, and full of promise—signaled the start of a new kind of freedom. A portal to somewhere else. Somewhere I might find people like me. It was exciting. Somewhere I didn't have to explain anything about my life, my parents, my identity. I didn't know exactly what I was searching for. I just knew it had to be out there, beyond my suburb, beyond my classroom, beyond what anyone around me could understand.

I plugged the phone line into the wall, waited for the connection, and signed into AOL (America Online). Hours slipped by in chat rooms, instant messages pinging between virtual strangers who became brief lifelines. I wasn't just passing time, I was testing my voice. Expressing a version of myself I couldn't show anyone in real life. That early internet, raw and clunky as it was, felt like a doorway to possibility.

At the same time, Melanie and I were filling the quiet with each other. We'd spend hours on the landline, the spiral cord stretching across the kitchen floor while we chattered about everything and nothing. I was trying hard, so hard, to be the typical American girl. The one who went to sleepovers with the white girls, who shared inside jokes, who laughed loud and easy. I wanted to be that carefree girl. I tried to become her. Even if deep down I still carried everything I wasn't. Everything I was pretending to be.

Melanie became my gateway to pop culture. We cut out posters from Teen Magazine, taping boy bands to our bedroom walls and debating which one we'd marry. I spent weeks saving coins, pedaling to the store just to buy the newest issue. I had a massive crush on Justin Timberlake from NSYNC and memorized every Britney Spears song religiously. After school, we raced home to catch *Total Request Live*, breathless to see which music video hit number one by popular vote. We squealed when our favorites made the countdown, hearts thudding as we imagined ourselves in the arms of the boys on screen.

But even in those harmless fantasies, I had a strange realization. None of those boys ever really ended up with girls who looked like me. In American music videos and on the red carpets of award shows, Asian girls weren't the ones being chased and sung about or on the arm of a celebrity.

But I kept pretending. I let myself dream, knowing even as I did that I was dreaming from the outside. Always watching. Always imagining myself in a world that didn't quite make space for us just yet.

Growing up, Hollywood's portrayal of Asians was narrow at best and often humiliating. If we weren't the awkward exchange student, we were the kung fu sidekick where our broken English was always the punchline. Our presence in the media was an exaggerated version of everything I was trying to downplay about who we were.

Then came *Mad TV*'s Mrs. Swan comedy skit. She was a white woman in a bowl-cut wig, squinting her eyes, draped in pale makeup to mimic a confused Asian woman speaking in a stilted, mocking accent. Every week, her skits played her off as dim-witted, unable to form a full sentence. Her most famous line, delivered with eyes half shut and that exaggerated voice, was, "He look-a like a man." Cue the laugh track. Cue the next day at school.

There was one episode I remember too clearly. Mrs. Swan is the victim of a robbery. A police officer asks for a description of the thief, and the entire skit becomes a drawn-out loop of her repeating the same line over and over. "He look-a like a man." That was the punchline. That was the whole joke. And the audience laughed like she was dumb as rocks.

I watched it, not knowing how I was supposed to feel. At first, I was just confused. Was it funny? Everyone else thought so, so I tried to laugh too. But I couldn't help but feel I was making fun of my Mom and Dad's generation, the generation of immigrants struggling with the language.

I didn't know how to respond to it. So I braced myself for school, knowing the lines would follow me. And they did. Kids mimicked her voice as I passed in the hallway, squinting their eyes, giggling. "He look-a like a man." Over and over. It felt like being dragged under a spotlight I never asked for.

I didn't have the words then to explain how harmful it was, how those roles the media fed us became the script kids used to mock me. They didn't see my parents. They saw caricatures. My fluent English didn't matter. The only lens they had was what they saw on

TV.

One evening Dad called me over to listen to the answering machine. He looked mad. I thought maybe Melanie had left a message for me to call her back, that maybe he was tired of us being on the phone too much. But when he pressed play, there was a message left by voices of young boys who made funny accents and laughed uncontrollably between each other. "Hello, this is for Mr. In-A-Thong, Ching Chong, Ching Chong!" I didn't even replay it. I furiously pressed the delete button. My Dad asked, "Who is that Ee-Lah?" I told him I didn't know, I told him it was some idiot.

Later it occurred to me, our school had passed around booklets with a directory of numbers. It included the school attendance line, teachers phone numbers, along with alphabetical names of students and their landlines. Kids often used the book to call their crushes and apparently, to make prank phone calls too. I was so upset, my face was red. It was one thing to tease and taunt me at school, but when it included my hardworking, harmless parents, it was a deeper kind of hurt to accept.

Things slowly shifted over time in the media. In the early 2000s, Lucy Liu stepped onto the screen as one of *Charlie's Angels*. She was a fierce, sexy, commanding Asian woman. It was the first time I saw someone who looked like me portrayed as powerful and desirable, not awkward or invisible. It felt like something was changing.

It took time before we saw actresses like Sandra Oh,

Awkwafina, Mindy Kaling—women who broadened the idea of what it meant to be Asian American. They were funny, complicated, smart, messy, and bold. They didn't fit into any one box.

Today, representation is finally increasing, like in Netflix's *Beef* and movies like *To All the Boys I've Loved Before*. It's a refreshing transition to see what everyday Asian Americans really look like. We are a variety of everyday people. Every time I see one of them on screen, I feel a little lighter, a little seen.

Some people might dismiss representation as surface-level. But when the world is constantly telling you what you are—foreign, submissive, a joke—people start to accept it. The media shaped how others saw me. It made me question how I saw myself. I guess I just wasn't living in the right time for it all to catch up.

For a time, I chased an impossible standard of beauty. I bought blue contact lenses and bleached thick, chunky blonde streaks into my hair, trying to look like Kelly Clarkson from American Idol. I looked like a skunk with black and white stripes. I was trying to be less foreign, more cool, more worthy.

It wasn't until high school that something started to shift in my environment.

High school was a bigger pond, drawing students from all over the district. For the first time, there were enough Asian kids to fill a cafeteria table. This was a huge change from my previous school, where there were only two of us in the entire building. That small circle became my refuge. I met girls from other nearby schools. Teenagers who were Vietnamese, Korean, Filipino, and even some Hmong. I was excited there were other kids born of Asian immigrants like me.

We spoke different dialects, our parents came from different villages, but we shared the same awkward memories of straddling two cultures. We laughed about the quirks only we could understand, like how our moms could call us fat one moment and insist we hadn't eaten enough the next. We swapped stories, compared our lives, and shared common grievances.

The Hmong kids and I even found a few common words between our languages, despite differences in tone and sound. It felt like we were uncovering secret bridges—proof that we were all connected, even in our differences.

Our tight-knit table didn't go unnoticed. Other kids asked why the Asian kids always sat together, as if our friendships were some sort of exclusionary club. There was something about our togetherness that made people uncomfortable. But we weren't loud or aggressive, we weren't even trying to make a statement. We were just trying to find common ground, to feel a little less alone in a world still figuring out how to make space for us.

Mai, my bold Hmong friend, would snap back, "Why don't they spread out too? We're not doing anything wrong!" She said what I often thought but was too afraid to voice. Of course, being high schoolers, everything felt high-stakes and dramatic. But underneath it all was a real desire to be understood and to belong without question.

I suspect Mai had her own insecurities. She used to cut tiny pieces of clear tape and stick them onto her eyelids, right above her lashes. "This makes your eyelids have a fold, so you get a crease and your eyes won't look so chinky," she'd say. "You're lucky, Amber, your eyes have a crease." I nodded. It was the first time in my young life someone told me that a feature of mine was actually desirable.

At the same time, Melanie and I began to drift apart. We still smiled at each other in the halls, but there was less to say between us. I was pulled toward this new community—a space where I didn't have to explain myself, where I didn't have to constantly translate who I was. My parents asked about Melanie often. They were worried, I think, about who I was becoming and the new crowd I had immersed myself in. Maybe they sensed I was changing, shedding the skin of the obedient daughter who used to linger on the sidelines.

I wanted to make room for all of me for once, not choosing between being Asian or American, but letting the two exist side by side. I stopped dying my hair. I stopped shrinking myself to fit in. I stopped trying to erase my roots.

For the first time, I felt a flicker of pride in who I was. It felt like I was finally getting somewhere like Mom's herbs in the backyard, rooted and quietly growing into the next season.

But just when I was finally starting to feel comfortable in my own skin, life had other plans. I couldn't have known then that the road ahead would unravel everything I thought I knew about myself, pushing me into places I never imagined I'd go.

By my second year of high school, everything started to spiral. I quickly learned that looking like I fit in on the outside didn't mean I was at home on the inside. Some of the new girls I hung out with lived fast and recklessly, and I wanted so badly to belong that I followed them down roads I probably shouldn't have.

Before long, I was skipping class, showing up at parties thrown by people who weren't even in school anymore. I dove deeper into things I knew I shouldn't—alcohol, pot, psychedelics and ecstasy. I knew a lot of teenagers go through phases like this, but I couldn't shake the feeling I was floating outside myself, watching from a distance as I slowly unraveled.

If I'd thought I was lost before, I had no idea how far I could drift from who I really was. I smoked in my bedroom once, unable to go outside because my brother was working on his car. I stupidly puffed through the cracked window, hoping the smell would vanish before my parents came home from work—the same hard-working parents who sacrificed everything to give me that room, that house, that life.

I'd wait until after 3:30 p.m. to intercept the school's automated calls reporting my absences, to stop whatever messages they'd leave on our machine. I spent my lunch money, the same money Dad handed to me with care each morning—on sneaking off campus, on mall trips with new friends, or convincing someone's older sibling to buy us cigarettes. It was utterly messed up.

Most weekends, I found myself at parties far from our bland suburb. Back then, party fliers were everywhere—bright scraps of paper with a date, time, and phone number, but no location until the last minute. We'd call just before the party, chasing the thrill of something bigger than us, something undefined.

I'd end up in rooms filled with music that felt unfamiliar—electronic, fast, pulsing—nothing like the pop and R&B I listened to alone in my bedroom.

One cold winter night, I found myself at a party in a run-down theater downtown, tucked away in a forgotten corner of Denver. The walls shook with bass. Strangers dissolved into strobe lights. The whole place pulsed with everyone's energy, but I was disconnected. My friends leaned in to shout over the music, but their words were swallowed by the noise. I stood there, dizzy from the smoke, the pounding sound, and something heavier, doubt. I was out of place all over again.

Then, through the haze, a woman walked in. She was an older Asian woman, flanked by a security guard, looking for her daughter. The girls around me burst out laughing. "Look, someone's mom is here!" they sneered.

I didn't laugh. I watched her from across the room, chest tight. I felt terrible for her. I wasn't any better than the girl she was searching for. My parents didn't know where I was either.

On the ride home, I stared out the window, the cold glass fogging with my breath. I felt like an idiot. I barely knew half the people in the car. We traded stories of immigrant parents, pressure, and identity struggles but none of it mattered. We were all chasing something, but I couldn't figure out what. Maybe we were all just lost in the same direction.

That night, I crept into the kitchen and warmed up the dinner Mom made. I sat alone at the table, high, trying to anchor myself to something familiar—maybe the food, maybe the normalcy of home.

When she came downstairs, her voice tired and soft, she asked, "Ee-Lah, where were you?"

I shrugged, not even looking at her. "Don't worry about it, Mom."

She didn't press. She just turned and went back upstairs.

I lay in bed that night, heavy with guilt. I hated what I'd become, the version of myself my parents couldn't recognize. I used to be the sweet girl who helped clean at their second jobs, who massaged their sore backs on weekends, who dressed up to go with Mom to the temple. Now, I was a stranger in my own home, pretending I didn't care. But I did. I just didn't know who I was anymore.

In the haze of those reckless nights, surrounded by people I shouldn't have been around, I eventually met him. He was a couple years older, didn't go to my school, didn't even live in my town. His parents were strict, immigrant Christians from El Salvador. But like me, he snuck out after they went to sleep. Before I knew it, I was spending my weekends running out to his old blue Toyota Corolla, heading off to the next party.

We never had a plan, just a shared desire for something we couldn't name. Some desperate need to feel happy about our life. I leaned on him more than I realized at the time. He made the parties feel less empty. I needed something to dull the gnawing discomfort that crept up inside me in those crowds. So I drank. I smoked. I kept going. We were lost together, and for a while, it made some sense.

When I was sixteen, I found myself sitting at the dining table in my parents' house, choking on a truth too heavy to swallow. I was pregnant.

We sat there. The four of us: my parents, him, and me, with eyes cast low, as if avoiding each other's gaze might delay the moment, might make it less real.

I don't remember who spoke first. The tension hung thick in the air, tangled in every breath. I couldn't tell who was more afraid, whether it was me, him, or my parents. But I saw the disappointment clear as day. They were stunned. I'd given them every reason to worry with slipping grades, failed classes, the unfamiliar crowd of friends, chasing fleeting moments at parties instead of building the future they dreamed for me. And there I was, confirmation that I was headed down a turbulent path.

Mom suggested we get engaged, but her words weren't born from romance. She was thinking of the Lao community, of what people would say, the whispers behind closed doors, the sideways glances she'd get at the temple. In our culture, shame doesn't belong to one person, it ripples through the whole family. Even if no one says a word, you feel it. You carry it.

His parents didn't agree. They were kind but firm: no wedding would happen just to save face. At the time, it felt like rejection. But now I know that it was protection. A rushed marriage wouldn't have saved us, it would've buried us in a bigger problem. That no was a gift in disguise.

In our small Lao community, people only celebrated the wins like honor rolls, graduations, scholarships, wedding invitations with gold trim. Everything else lived in the shadows. Addiction. Divorce. Debt. Teenage pregnancy. We all knew it existed, but it never made it past the front porch. I was becoming one of those secrets. And I felt painfully guilty for putting my parents in that position.

A few days later, Saeng came over. She didn't scold me or raise her voice. She just sat at the edge of my bed, sighed, and said my name so softly it tore through me: "Amber…" I burst into tears. Jay came by too. His concern was sharper, more direct. His words weren't cruel, but they carried weight. "Are you sure you're going to be ready for this?" Of course I wasn't. Not yet. At night, I lay in bed, four weeks pregnant and already sleepless, already spinning in the gravity of a future I wasn't sure I was ready for, but couldn't walk away from either.

When the house was dark and still, the child in me slipped out of my room and tiptoed toward the family

Buddha display. The soft glow from the cabinet light bathed the small gold statue in a warm, peaceful light. Buddha's eyes were closed, hands resting gently in his lap—still, serene. I knelt on the carpet and stared. I didn't know how to pray for this. I didn't know what words to say, because what I was going through wasn't something taught at the temple. I didn't ask for anything, I just sobbed. I cried like the child I still was, aching for an answer, but none came.

The next day, Mom approached me softly, her voice gentle as she tried to ease my fears. "Ee-Lah, I want to tell you about a dream I had last night..." I listened intently, curious about what she felt so compelled to share and eager for any distraction from the weight of recent news.

She began with a story about her mother, the strong woman who once moved her and her siblings to Houayxay all those years ago.

Mom painted a vivid picture of the dream. It began with her opening the front doors of our suburban home to look outside. There was a truck parked in the driveway, and her brother emerged from the driver's seat. Mom asked what he was doing there, and he walked around to the passenger side and opened the door. To her surprise, their mother came out of the car, looking small, fragile, and old. She didn't speak in the dream. Her brother explained that their mother wanted to stay with her. She had missed so many years with Mom after immigrating to America.

Mom asked how that could be, since their mother

had passed away years before. But her brother had no answer. "She just... wants to be with you. You need to let her be with you," he said.

Mom woke from the dream with a confusing message to decipher.

She was full of joy when she explained reincarnation, a belief in Buddhism. She was certain the dream was a sign that her mother wanted to be near her still, even after death. She believed my pregnancy was a reincarnation of her mother, a chance to live her next life through my child.

Though I wasn't sure what to make of Mom's belief, I couldn't deny that it was a beautiful way to see our new circumstances. So I hugged her and told her, "Maybe it is so."

Something inside me had settled. Fueled by determination and the promise to do everything I possibly could, I began preparing for the next chapter of my life. I started searching for resources, making phone calls, looking for help and eventually, I found it: a program for teen mothers trying to finish high school. It was in Boulder, the very city where I was born. A strange kind of full circle. Maybe not the one I'd imagined, but a circle nonetheless.

The teen parent program was small and housed within a general high school. As a result, most of the students there were not expectant parents. But downstairs, tucked away in the basement, were three nurseries, each divided by age: newborns, infants, and toddlers. Each morning, a small group of teen parents would drop off their babies and diaper bags before heading upstairs to class. When I officially enrolled, there would be nine of us—nine young mothers juggling algebra tests and midnight feedings alike.

By the time my junior year started, I was attending classes in my second and third trimester of pregnancy. I'd hoped to share classes with some of the other moms, but we were all at different academic levels, needing different credits to graduate. We ended up with no classes together. So there I was sitting in math class, my belly barely fitting behind the desk, surrounded by whispers and judgmental stares from other teens I didn't know.

The temptation to skip class crept in more than once, but I refused to give in. What kept me going was the knowledge that somewhere else in that school, eight other young mothers were fighting their own battles in their own classrooms. We were all a little embarrassed, sleep-deprived, and exhausted. But deep down, I knew I was exactly where I needed to be. No matter how ashamed I felt or how hard it was, I kept my butt in that chair. That was the start of my new beginning.

The program helped by donating used baby items. I was lucky enough to find sheets for a crib, tiny clothes, and other essentials that made this new life a little easier.

I applied for W.I.C. A government assistance for women, infants, and children, to help pay for formula and food. I was slowly and clumsily, inching forward.

On July 15th, I woke up before sunrise, drenched in the thick heat of summer in our house with no air conditioning. Painful cramps gripped me while everyone else was still asleep. Carefully, I got out of bed and crept down the noisy plastic-covered stairs to the kitchen, hoping a bowl of MAMA brand ramen noodles would calm my stomach. That morning, I couldn't even finish it. The pain didn't ease.

Forty minutes later, I was on my way to the hospital. At 2:20 pm, Kaela entered the world. I still joke about how everyone rushed to crowd around her glass incubator while I lay alone on the hospital bed. Alone and trembling with adrenaline, dizzy from everything that had unfolded in those eight hours.

Mom and Dad held her with a joy that needed no words. Saeng gently placed her hand on my arm and told me, "You did a great job." Jay didn't arrive until later, he was working a shift as a delivery boy at a Chinese restaurant at the time. But when he finally got there, he handed me a card he'd made by cutting out the Chinese zodiac from the takeout menu. It was for the Year of the Monkey, listing personality traits, characteristics, and future predictions for my new little girl. I cried. Yes, this was our new addition to the family, born in the Year of the Monkey.

In those brief moments of welcoming Kaela, everything shifted in our family. There's no way to truly explain what happens when you hold your child for the first time unless you've lived it. Something in your brain chemistry switches, it's like a door opens inside your heart you never knew existed. She was so small with a full head of hair and perfect, I couldn't believe I had brought her into the world. From that moment, nothing else mattered to me. Nothing about who I was, who was okay with me, or where I belonged. This was the path laid out for me, my purpose became clear.

That fall, still healing from breastfeeding, I stepped into my last year of high school. Each morning, I packed my backpack alongside Kaela's diaper bag. I buckled her into her car seat and drove us both to school Monday through Friday in Dad's old maroon Toyota 4-Runner. He still gave me lunch money, just like he always had, and I used it for gas and a sandwich each day.

At school, I didn't sit with anyone at lunch. Instead, I joined Kaela in the basement nursery, or if she was sleeping in one of the cribs, I'd eat alone in my car to avoid disturbing her. It got lonely sometimes in that car, I felt like I was missing out on being a teen, but I eventually learned to stop caring. Soon, what once felt like the biggest deal, having friends to eat lunch with, felt trivial. I had new priorities to focus on. I showed up day to day, tired but determined, ready to face whatever came next.

In May of 2005, Kaela was just ten months old when I walked across that stage, dressed in my red cap and gown. It was well-earned after a jam-packed schedule of classes, including a math class at night throughout my senior year. By some miracle, I graduated high school right on time, not a single day late. Of the 502 graduates that year, nine were teen moms. We were just a microscopic fraction of the class. We wore a special silk purple cord draped over our gowns as a symbol of every challenge we had faced and overcome. When honors students with gold cords asked what the purple cords meant, we spoke with pride when we said, it was for teen mother graduates.

Back at home, Mom and Dad opened our doors to friends and community members for a traditional Baci ceremony. It was a celebration woven with love and promise. The room was filled with monks and elders who gently tied white cotton strings around our wrists. Each string was a blessing, meant to bring luck, prosperity, and protection from harm. They tied strings around both Kaela's and my wrists until the cords overlapped, too many to count. The ceremony was healing, a soft but powerful promise of a better future.

Kaela's arrival brought our family closer in ways I hadn't imagined possible. Our days became filled with shared meals I wanted so badly as a kid, more laughter, and watching her tiny hands grasp the world around her. After graduation, I worked full-time and took college classes at night, always moving forward. There was no room to pause, no luxury to hesitate. I was building a life for Kaela and secretly, still trying with every ounce of my being to make my parents proud.

By the time Kaela turned three, her father and I eventually parted ways. We were both so young. He wasn't truly ready to be a family man or to take on the journey we had started together. His grip on the past—the parties, the freedom—created a fracture between us that time never fully healed.

My parents became a large part of helping me raise Kaela. Despite their initial concerns for me and the weight of community shame, they became my strongest support. Kaela's birth drew us closer in new and beautiful ways. My sister, who once only visited on holidays and occasional drop-ins, began asking to take Kaela for weekends at her condo. Dad found an old camcorder and started recording her first year, month by month. He said it was so we could look back and see how quickly she was growing, but I knew it was his way of holding onto every little moment.

Mom and Dad lit up in a way I'd never seen before. Maybe it was because Kaela was their first granddaughter, something they hadn't yet imagined. Mom would pop her head into my room faster than I could lift my head whenever Kaela stirred in the night. She loved helping with baths, feeding her tiny spoonfuls of food, and smiling as she gently squeezed Kaela's chubby thighs. True to her Lao roots, Mom even tried to adorn Kaela with delicate gold bracelets that jingled softly whenever she moved.

Dad made silly voices through the camcorder's lens, his faint laughter audible in the background. He was the first to teach her how to ride her bike without training wheels while I was at work. Those moments warmed my heart in ways words can barely capture, a steady reminder that even in unpredictable times, love finds its way home.

Somewhere along the way, my parents stopped carrying the weight of the Lao community's judgment.

The shame that once shadowed our lives began to loosen its grip, replaced by something more important—their focus on Kaela's happiness, her health, and the sound of her laughter filling our home like a new kind of prayer. I suppose Mom and Dad had their own hurdle to overcome, breaking free from their old cultural mindset to embrace something new, something less traditional. That shift wasn't just theirs, it was ours together. A slow evolution of hope and healing.

Back then, there wasn't much time for reflection. I just kept moving forward, juggling everything: being a mom, earning money, working toward a degree, trying to maintain a social life with friends and have a boyfriend. Some moments were beautiful, others were tough, it was a constant wave of highs and lows.

I helped Kaela with her homework, tucked her into bed, then stayed up late reading syllabi and writing term papers when I was exhausted. We made poster boards for school projects, crafted Halloween costumes, and learned the meaning of growing up side by side.

I made it a priority to chaperone her school field trips and, eventually, took her to work on Take Your Child to Work Day—just as Mom had done for me years before. This time, Kaela got to experience an office filled with computers and games.

Looking back, I realize I was hard on her. I relied on Kaela to be a reflection of how I was as a parent, scolding her over math homework just like my dad once did. Some habits, I suppose, I picked up from my parents without even noticing.

As life unfolded, I faced many of the same struggles my parents did, trying to figure out how to provide for us. Though I knew my parents could always help, my pride kept me from asking. There were times when the lights got turned off at our apartment, and when I struggled just to buy groceries. I still carry the guilt from those moments with Kaela. She eventually grew into a conscientious little girl, who never asked for things we couldn't afford. Looking out for us in her own little way.

When Kaela hit her teenage years, I feared for a moment she might follow the same troubled path I had. But she surprised me in ways I never imagined. She grew into such a responsible, grounded person, with an old soul. I guess maybe Mom was onto something about reincarnation after all.

The bond Kaela and I share was forged in struggle and growing pains. I believe it's stronger because I had her when I was so young. We faced so much together, learned from each other, and figured it all out. We were both still kids navigating life for the first time.

If my work ethic was a gift from my parents, Kaela was the one who shaped it into something real. She made me stronger. She made me want more, for her and for both of us. Suddenly, I had a bigger purpose, a fire that burned steady and clear. I got better jobs after finishing college. And after years of moving between apartments, we finally bought our first home when she turned 13—a place where we could grow up steadily. A small victory.

Soon, in the blink of an eye, her turn came. I found myself sitting in that same Boulder auditorium, watching Kaela walk across the high school graduation stage I once stood on. She wore her cap and gown with grace. I didn't cry, but I sat there filled with something deeper than pride. When they called her name, I stood and shouted as loud as I could.

My family and I hadn't just raised a daughter, we raised a young woman with a future. A future where she would never have to worry about the safety of her home or the decision to escape or leave any of us behind.

We held the infamous Baci ceremony again at my parents' home—a blessing for her journey, a tradition renewed, and a circle that keeps turning.

I'm often reminded of the girl I used to be—the one who shrank at questions about Laos, who flushed with embarrassment at my parents' accents, who just wanted to disappear to make everyone else comfortable with me. I wasted so much time trying to change for people, not realizing how much of myself I was pushing away.

Living with those little regrets, I wanted to shield Kaela from the things I felt growing up. I reminded her often to take pride in her culture and heritage. We talk openly about where we come from with Mom and Dad, and we work hard to instill pride in both her Lao and Salvadoran roots. She danced in Lao New Year celebrations throughout her childhood, until she outgrew the role at 18. Her dad threw her a proper quinceañera when she turned 15, a beautiful tradition of their own.

Today, Kaela is 21. A young woman with her own dreams, her own path stretching out ahead. It still feels surreal how fast the years have flown by. It scares me how quickly time passes before my eyes.

These days, you can find all of us gathered around the table with Mom. Cooking traditional Lao meals together keeps our stories alive and honors the history that shaped us. My silent wish is that Kaela carries our legacy forward, a legacy born from a small Lao family who traveled far across the river and ocean to build a new life here.

My parents filled our home with customs and traditions, no matter how much I resisted them. And granted for a time, I slowly disappeared from temple visits, stopped speaking the language at home, and avoided the parts of me that felt too different. But with motherhood and with a new sense of respect, I began to understand. I saw my parents not just as Mom and Dad, but as immigrants who carried the weight of a future they wanted to give us, a chance at something better.

I suppose the older I got, the more I wanted to honor that in all the right ways. I wanted to understand them not just for myself, but so I could pass their values on to Kaela in a way that felt honest and authentic.

There is something deeply healing in finally embracing the culture I once tried to hide. Rejecting it left me hollow, like I was only living a fraction of who I was meant to be. The truth is, when we spend our lives trying to fit in, we risk losing the very parts that make us whole.

If we let that continue, if each generation drifts a little further from themselves, we risk losing it all. The language stops being spoken, and the culture fades. The recipes stop simmering on the stove. The holidays, the stories, and the rituals slip away. My parents knew this. Even when I didn't see it, the temple visits, the traditions, and the food held so much more meaning. They were roots, grounding us in a history and a resilience that refused to be forgotten.

I wish I'd recognized it sooner, and accepted myself earlier. But maybe that is the work of being first-generation—the slow, sometimes turbulent journey of finding your place between two worlds. Maybe it just takes time.

6 | Present Day

When my parents retired after 23 years of service, the university honored them with engraved plaques. Saeng organized and hosted a celebration at a local hall where she gave a heartfelt speech to Mom and Dad. "I remember when me, Mom, and Dad saw snow for the first time..." she began, circling back to their first experience in Washington.

The Lao community gathered to dance, share food, and rejoice. It was a beautiful milestone reached. After decades of hard work, there was finally a long-awaited sigh of relief.

One of the first things Mom and Dad did with their newfound freedom was plan a trip to Seattle—to visit the Hansons and reunite with the family who sponsored them all those years ago.

The night before their flight, Mom laid out her clothes with the care and attention of someone preparing for a wedding—each piece folded just right, every detail considered.

My dad, who never fussed over appearances, polished his shoes until they shone.

"It's been so long," Mom muttered, her voice tinged with both excitement and worry. "What if they don't recognize us?" I told her that was highly unlikely, and we both shared a laugh.

The most significant moments in life don't always come with grand gestures or loud celebrations.

Sometimes, they happen in a kitchen filled with the aroma of tea and in shared stories that stretch across decades. Mom and Dad were honoring a promise—one made to themselves, to the past they carried, and to the life they had painstakingly built here through years of struggle and perseverance.

Once, they feared telling anyone who they were. Now, they have built a legacy that ensures those memories live on, weaving through our family like a steady thread.

When they arrived in Seattle, the Hanson family's address was nowhere to be found. So my parents retraced their earliest steps, making their way to the small Lutheran church where they had first attended services with the Hansons after arriving in America.

The church hadn't changed much—the weathered white siding, the stained-glass windows catching the morning light, the wooden sign out front worn by decades of sun and rain. They stepped inside cautiously, hearts fluttering with the weight of old memories and the goal of reconnection.

The pastor at the church was young, but empathetic and understanding. After hearing their story, he searched through the church's archives and, against the odds, he found a record for Mr. Hanson. A call was made and an address was shared.

Mr. Hanson had moved from the original home Mom and Dad first arrived at, but still lived in Washington. Soon, my parents stood before an unfamiliar house nestled in a neighborhood in between pine trees. They were clutching a box of small gifts and photos of me and my siblings—a lifetime compressed into snapshots.

When the door opened, there stood Mr. Hanson—older now, his frame more frail. For a moment, recognition flickered across his face like a light returning after a long absence. "I can't believe it," he answered, before pulling them into an embrace that seemed to pause time itself.

His welcome was warm and unchanging, the kind of kindness that endures beyond years and distance. Tears were shed, embraces lingered, and words of gratitude filled the room.

Inside, the house smelled of fresh coffee and lemon polish, familiar and comforting. Photographs of his children and grandchildren lined the mantle—a testament to the life he continued to build after Mom and Dad had moved on.

They sat together as they once had so many years ago, around a smaller table where simple meals were shared—casseroles, stews, salad, and warm bread fresh from the oven. Only this time, they were not strangers or newcomers to the land. They were survivors, family, bound by a shared history and an unspoken understanding of what it meant to be given a second chance.

They flipped through old photos—some faded with time, others crisp and vivid. My parents showed him pictures of graduations, weddings, and baby Kaela. They were grandparents now, storytellers and legacy builders.

Mr. Hanson listened with pride and amazement, shaking his head at how swiftly the years had passed and how the family evolved beyond ways he dreamed of. He confessed he hadn't kept in touch with many of the families he helped sponsor, life pulling him forward as it always does.

The visit was a pilgrimage back to the roots of their second chance. That humble house, that warm meal, that familiar face—embodied everything they had worked for and sacrificed to create themselves. It was their own full-circle moment, fragile and powerful, held together by gratitude and the joy of belonging.

They had come so far. From fleeing war-torn Laos with nothing but fragile resolve, to raising children in a country whose language once felt like an impenetrable wall, they were now able to say: we made it. This visit was their way of honoring that long, winding journey—a gesture of deep gratitude to the man who had opened the door for them all those years ago.

Though Mom and Dad had returned to Laos time and again before and after retirement—each trip a stirring reunion with family and a reconnection to the land of their birth—this visit to Seattle was something far different. It was a testament to the very start of their American story. A declaration that said: We remember. We never forgot. And we never will.

As my parents aged over the years, my responsibilities began to increase. It was my duty to. I guess in my own little way, it was also an act of service to repay my debt to them. After their retirement, I went on to manage more of their advanced doctors appointments and do their taxes. There were specialists they couldn't understand and medical jargon that they still had to adapt to. I see their ongoing challenge to keep up with a world that's moving faster than they can keep up with.

I also gained a larger respect and perspective on immigrants in America—by people who dared to dream, who rebuilt their lives from scratch. Because I watched my parents do just that. I don't think I'll ever fully know what it feels like to learn how to live in an unfamiliar place that offers freedom but demands so much from you in return.

I asked Mom what the hardest part of those early years were. She paused, and said it was the feeling of invisibility—like all their sacrifices and hard work went unnoticed, unappreciated. She spoke of the loneliness that crept in as she moved through empty offices and silent hallways, her hands busy with work while her heart ached for home, wondering about her brothers and sisters in Laos.

I reminded her gently that she was never invisible—that I saw her, that Saeng and Jay saw her. We saw both of their labor in the calluses on their hands and the weariness in their eyes. We saw the hurdles—the barriers, the cultural misunderstandings—that she climbed every day with Dad, even in the simplest tasks like grocery shopping or asking for directions.

She smiled and her face softened a bit, as she remembered something else—the bright moments among the struggle. She spoke of the immigrant women she worked with, many from South America and Mexico, who became more than coworkers—they became sisters in struggle. Together, they shared lunches filled with family recipes, traded stories of their faraway homelands, and swapped tamales for egg rolls or sticky rice wrapped in banana leaves. In those quiet exchanges, they found community in a place no matter how foreign.

She recalled the neighbor who asked about our Lao recipes during one of our celebrations. Mom invited her in to share a plate, she loved our food. From that moment on, something changed. She started bringing egg rolls and fried rice to the neighbor, little gifts that carried pride and a growing sense of acceptance. "I bring to her, because I know she like it." Mom smiled. Those little friendships and gestures were something Mom never expected to find here, but in time, she did.

And that's what we went on to discover over the years—a mixture of moments, some of which came from being unseen one moment and learning about people in another. We found things we never expected. We learned more about who we were becoming. Defining what being Asian-American looks like day by day.

I'm grateful for having Colorado as our steady home. The Rocky Mountains will always have a special place in my heart—familiar and grounding. They were a part of me long before I ever ventured beyond our small suburb. The memories of riding my bike to school in the dry, crisp air are ones I hold close. It was the one constant that kept me grounded in a world that often felt uncertain.

I had the privilege of growing up in the steady rhythm of the seasons, each one bringing its own comfort and grace. Every change marked the passage of time—the ski season blanketing the peaks in snow, autumn's fiery leaves lining the streets, and early mornings spent hiking to catch the sunrise. I'm lucky to still enjoy that life today.

I watched Denver transform beyond recognition. The city continued to bring new faces, more jobs, more buildings over the years. It's a place that draws people in from everywhere, each with their own dreams and hunger for something better. Although, I haven't run into anyone I went to school with. Maybe they've moved, or maybe the city is just full of newcomers. But Denver, once my familiar home, is now full of a beautiful blend of people whose lives make up what it's become.

With all its rapid growth, I hold onto the expectation that the variety of people moving here continues. That a Lao restaurant will open here someday. Because food is more than just sustenance; it's a true reflection of a city's diversity. Major cities across the U.S. get to thrive on flavors from every corner of the world, with each dish telling its own unique story. I'd only experienced Lao food in places like California and Minnesota, where the Asian community is more prominent—a luxury I could only dream of as a child. A Lao restaurant here would not only honor our heritage but also enrich the city's cultural tapestry, celebrating the beauty of blending traditions and experiences.

As life unfolded before me and my career developed, it was worlds apart from the jobs Mom and Dad had to do. I went on, never having to endure the physically demanding work they did. I climbed corporate ladders, stayed up late studying for licensing exams, discovered my voice through writing, and stumbled through the fast-paced world of advertising. Each job taught me something new, each moment a sprint—a race to prove myself, to make something of my life. It's pretty incredible to have those kinds of opportunities.

Perhaps my parents felt something similar, but in their own way. Their lives were full of relentless decisions—each one life-altering and demanding everything from them. With little choice but to keep going.

Even as a Lao-American woman I still find myself pulled in different directions—torn between the values of my traditional upbringing and the more modern beliefs of the society I live in.

My Lao parents were my biggest example. Two people who've stayed married through displacement, hunger, poverty, and dug their way to a more sustainable life. I developed a strong sense of commitment to the institution of marriage. It's something I deeply believe in—an enduring bond that can withstand the years, the challenges, and the quiet struggles. But in a society that's become increasingly skeptical of marriage, where more people are opting out of long-term commitments, I've found that belief harder to hold onto.

There are traditional roles and values that I carry with me—traits and expectations I believe should remain in the role of a wife, shaped by what I observed in Mom's example growing up. Moms unwavering dedication to our family, her sense of duty and care, created a blueprint for what I imagined my future might look like.

Yet, at the same time, my circumstances pushed me to become a woman who fiercely values her independence. My career ambitions, my desire to build something for myself—that were born out of the need to thrive in America, especially as a single mom navigating the complexities of raising a daughter on my own. I learned early on how to stand on my own two feet, to carve my own path, and to protect my own sense of self.

And so, I live with a different kind of tug-of-war these days. A tension between wanting to honor the traditions I was raised with, and a modern drive to shape my own future on my terms. It's a balancing act I'm still trying to figure out.

Today, we get to be part of a place where we have the freedom to be ourselves. It's messy and imperfect, but it's a far cry from what we ever would have been able to achieve in Laos. Here, we get to shape our identities, express our beliefs, argue, protest, and demand change.

Of course, even with all that, America has a difficult political landscape. We had to accept that freedom comes with its costs. It brings challenges—fear, hatred, division. We see it in how immigrants are treated and in the dangers posed by our differences. It's hard not to feel it, especially when you're still considered foreign in a place you're meant to call home.

For the Asian American community as a whole, the COVID 19 pandemic stripped away a lot of things, but it also exposed the ugliness of xenophobia. The virus became a weapon in the hands of hate, and suddenly, the language of racism seemed louder, more dangerous.

When the COVID 19 travel restrictions finally lifted, I was given a special gift to visit Seattle for a short birthday weekend. While I didn't get to see everyone I wanted (like our sponsors), the trip felt important in ways I couldn't quite explain. I was lucky to be able to visit the very city Mom and Dad first arrived in. I had not experienced it yet, as I wasn't born until a later chapter of my parents' lives.

After a beautiful meal at a Cambodian restaurant, I made my way toward the bus to spend the rest of the evening at the waterfront, wanting to take in the city and explore more.

But as I crossed a busy street, caught up in the rush of getting to the bus stop, a man was walking toward me in the opposite direction. He was mumbling, wrapped in layers of blankets, his words almost slurred, incoherent. As we got close enough to cross paths on the crosswalk, he aggressively shouted two words at me—sharp and hateful—that hit me with the force of a punch: "Chinese bitch!"

I was unprepared and caught off guard. It was like my spirit froze as my legs continued walking. My throat closed, my chest tight, I was taken aback by the shock. It stung me raw. I told myself to breathe, to stay calm and keep walking. But even as I caught up to the bus afterward, I sat down gently and felt the red burn in my cheeks, the tears that threatened their way up to my eyes. I was 35 years old, I had to keep it together. I inhaled and refused to let any tears fall.

I was reminded later of how I didn't stand up for myself that night. I didn't say a word. But in that moment the little girl in me took over and I kept my mouth shut yet again. I pretended to let it go, but it stayed with me, that feeling. The shame. The hurt.

I didn't realize how bad things were until the trip I took to Seattle post COVID 19. Until the stranger who chopped me down to nothing, when I was merely crossing the street.

I thought of my parents, I grew worried for them, watching the violence escalate towards Asian-Americans in the news. But just like every other time, we had to remain brave and hopeful as we watched the world continue to unfold.

Still, my parents have never wavered in their belief that America is a work in progress, and remained the best place for us to keep on trying.

As my daughter grows up in this new world that's learning how to embrace the layers of complexity in identity, and grappling with its own biases—I am still relieved she's living in this moment of time. Because she's grown up in a time to witness and speak about movements like Black Lives Matter, the chaos of the COVID-19 pandemic, and the divisive political landscape that follows each election.

This is a time where mixed-race children like her, are becoming more visible each day. As a second-generation Asian-Latina young woman, she has the space to wear her identity with pride, never shrinking, and never apologizing for who she is. Kaela is strong and I watched her move through with a confidence I never had. Evolving into the woman I dreamed she'd always become—unyielding, thoughtful, and proud of who she is. In many ways, she teaches me more than I ever taught her.

We've made a commitment to stop the generational shame. When someone asks where Laos is, we proudly share our story, our history. And if they ask about our food, we welcome them to our kitchen.

Now, Colorado has remained our family's anchor. Saeng, who once lived in holding areas and battled illness in refugee camps, walks a professional career path with brilliance and grace that she can be proud of. Jay, still a loyal Seattle Seahawks sports fan, leads his life with steadiness and independence exploring different states. I found my way—finishing graduate school, raising Kaela as a single mom, and carving out a career I'm still shaping. And Kaela is attending classes at the very same university where Mom and Dad worked. Now, preparing to walk across the stage for the second time, she's about to receive her first college degree.

WHAT WE BROUGHT ACROSS THE RIVER

The way our family's story has unfolded over the decades says everything. From the refugee camps to a quiet suburb in Colorado, from survival to living—we've come so far, yet somehow, it feels like we're still just beginning.

It's a legacy that stretches from my parents' sacrifices, through my own experiences, and now into Kaela's future. I see the fruits of their labor. I see how their dreams have taken shape, how our family has become more than they ever imagined.

And it's not just about the milestones—their citizenship, the degrees we earned, the careers, or the homes we've settled into—it's about the invisible links that connect us. The quiet moments, the little wins, the times we learned from each other when everything else felt uncertain. We got through them together.

With Kaela standing on the precipice of her own future, it will be up to her to carry this legacy forward in her own way. She won't be bound by the same limitations my parents encountered. Yet, she'll be shaped by them like I was. Her future isn't just hers—it's ours, too. It's the future we fought for, the future only dreamed of when they first arrived, unsure of where we'd land but wishful that we could make it.

We are all part of the same evolving story—one that's still being written. We are building a passage from our past to our future—an evolution of protection, resilience, and dreams. And our story, our journey, will be something we carry on forever.

AMBER D. INTHAVONG

7 | Return to the Motherland

The plane jolted as its wheels rolled onto the runway, a brief, bumpy embrace before gliding smoothly forward. Outside, the January sun beamed in the humid thick jungle air, a stark contrast to the dry Rockies I knew so well. My fingers hesitated on the window shade before I pulled it up, heart pounding with a mix of excitement and anticipation. Then, over the fuzzy speaker came the words I'd waited years to hear: "Ladies and gentlemen, welcome to Laos."

A thrill swept through me, like stepping into a dream both familiar and strange. I reached for my phone and earbuds, then turned to Kaela, catching her eyes with a smile full of meaning. "We're here," I leaned over. "Are you ready?"

Around us, the cabin buzzed with restless energy, passengers eager to leave the cramped space behind. Usually, the shuffle would annoy me, but this time, I shared it—the impatience of returning to the motherland, of finally arriving where our story began. The scent of earth and rain and something ancient clung to the air as we moved toward the exit, thick and alive in a way that no mountain breeze ever was.

Stepping outside, I breathed it all in—the heat, the smells, the life pulsing from the land itself. This was the place where my parents' journey had started, a place I carried inside me but had never truly understood. As a child, I hated Laos—the oppressive heat, the relentless insects, the overwhelming crowd of relatives. I wasn't ready then to hold its weight.

But now, standing here with Kaela by my side, and my parents just behind us, I came back with a new purpose—one shaped by time, by love, and by the fierce desire to reclaim a heritage I once tried to hide. This was not just a visit. It was a proper homecoming.

I wasn't entirely sure what I was searching for—answers, maybe, or clarity. Just a better grip on our heritage. All I knew was that something inside me ached to feel whole, and I believed Laos held the missing pieces. This time, I was a grown woman, returning after decades in the making.

Inside Vientiane's airport, the stickiness clung to my skin as ceiling fans spun lazily overhead, barely offering relief. The rhythmic flow of voices in Lao and English filled the crowded space. Young men in green uniforms stood behind counters, their faces unreadable as they processed the endless stream of travelers.

One customs officer stepped forward, his voice polite but firm. "What hotel are you staying at? What is the purpose of your visit?" I handed over my paperwork, trying to steady my hands. He scanned it quickly, then smiled and motioned me toward a different line. "Right this way."

At that moment, it struck me how much it had taken to arrive here. The months of working extra shifts, the careful saving of every dollar. But this trip was bigger than my own yearning to reconnect. It was a gift to my parents—another reunion years in the waiting. For my father, a chance to hug his mother once more. For Kaela, a second-generation Lao-American, the first glimpse of the land that carried our history.

We had planned every detail. Two weeks with family, making up for time lost. Two weeks exploring ancient temples and the landscapes that shaped my parents' childhoods.

The airport erupted into a lively chaos as we stepped outside. Taxis lined up like eager performers, drivers calling out, bargaining loudly, the energy raw and immediate. Unlike back home, where a ride is summoned with a tap on a phone screen app, here connection was personal, verbal, human.

Dad took charge, leading us to the currency exchange counter. American bills traded for bright stacks of yellow and pink Lao Kip—colors so vivid they looked almost fake, yet heavy with meaning in the hands of the teller.

Our taxi driver, an older man with a wide toothy smile, insisted on lifting our six suitcases himself. Mom's luggage overflowed with gifts—clothes, handbags, small luxuries for relatives who had far less. She had always said you never come home empty-handed. Even when money was tight, sending care across the ocean was a meaningful act, a thread tying us back to family, to home.

As we drove through the streets, my father's easy conversation with the taxi driver faded into the background. My eyes took in the world rushing past the window—bustling open-air markets, golden temples shimmering in the afternoon light, street vendors fanning smoky charcoal fires. Every detail was new and alive, a vivid tapestry of sights and sounds that both thrilled and unsettled me.

By the time we reached our hotel, exhaustion tugged at our bones, but hunger quickly overpowered it. We stepped outside, guided by the rich scent of grilled meats and steaming rice wafting through the hot air. Around a corner, a small vendor's stall caught my attention—a man and a woman expertly chopping fresh Lao sausage into bite-sized pieces, the fragrant aroma of lemongrass rising.

The smell struck a chord deep inside me—the same scent that once filled our kitchen back home when Mom made sausage from scratch. I could still see myself at that dining table, stuffing pork into casings, my little fingers aching from the effort. Back then, it was just a chore. Now, I crave every bite of it.

Dad ordered for us, and we settled onto plastic stools by the dusty roadside. The cook swung a machete with practiced ease, splitting open a coconut and letting its juice spill over his hands before handing it to us. Kaela, wearing oversized sunglasses, took a tentative sip. I snapped a photo, desperate to capture the moment—to hold on to the weight of this place. Dad let out a contented, "Ahhh." That familiar sound, the one that once used to annoy me at home. But here, it felt different. It felt right.

I was filled with joy to see Mom and Dad in their element. No one treated them as if they were unintelligent or incapable here. It was just how it should be.

News of our arrival traveled fast. My Aunt Pah Tee came rushing to greet us. She was Mom's older sister. She once tried to speak English to me when I was a child, on our last visit, years before. Her effort was a small gift that lingered in my memory ever since.

Tears filled her eyes as she wrapped us in a fierce embrace, her warmth and laughter filling the space around us like a light. She turned to Kaela, marveling at her mixed features—half Lao, half Salvadoran. I saw the curiosity in her gaze as she traced Kaela's face, as if searching for the threads of family woven into her.

Watching Pah Tee, I realized how much she resembled Mom—the same face, the same voice, even the same laugh. Yet their lives had been shaped by different worlds. Mom, with her porcelain skin and designer handbag, molded by decades in America. Pah Tee, weathered and sun-kissed, a woman of the earth and the land. For the first time, I wondered what Mom's life might have been like if she had stayed—raising bulls on a farm instead of navigating a mop through classrooms and hallways. Did Pah Tee ever wonder what might have been? Did Mom carry guilt for leaving? But I didn't ask. Instead, I watched as they clung to one another, laughter spilling easily between them. At that moment, I understood: maybe they had already let go of those questions long ago.

Luang Prabang (Long-Pra-Bang) became my favorite place on this journey. It was a beautiful village with an explosion of color and life nestled beneath the towering green mountains. Mom said they never got to visit Luang Prabang as a kid, they couldn't afford to. It was a special place where the King of Laos once lived and growing up she had only heard about it in school. But there we were, returning as visitors, and able to see Luang Prabang now that she was much older, with her grown daughter and grandchild.

We came across the King's palace, only it was standing now as a museum, with barriers roped off to prevent tourists from entering. "Grandpa, why doesn't the King live there anymore?" Kaela asked, "Shh! Don't say anything about the King when we're here Kaela."

All these years later and Dad still feared them. Still feared our conversations would be heard by the communists. The worry never left him, that feeling we'd get into trouble for even questioning why the country wasn't a monarchy anymore.

The streets in Luang Prabang pulsed with energy and people, the buildings painted in warm hues that seemed to glow against the lush landscape. Climbing the steep steps of Mount Phousi felt like a rite of passage. The midday sun pressed down, heavy and unrelenting, but when we reached the summit, the world unfolded beneath us like a sacred tapestry. Villages stretched out in golden light, the roofs and gardens small and perfect against the vastness of the sky.

At the base, village women sold tiny birds cradled in delicate woven cages—just a dollar each. We each took one in our hands as we began the climb, hearts full of joy. At the top, we released them into the air, with silent prayers that carried on the breeze. My bird paused for a heartbeat, as if hesitating between my hands, before bursting into flight and disappearing into the endless blue. It was a simple act, but in that moment, it felt like a bridge—an unspoken message: I am here. I remember. I honor what came before.

That night, the night market came alive with colors, sounds, and scents. The air was fragrant with sizzling spices and sweet herbs, mingling with the laughter and chatter of vendors and visitors. When we saw the banner for *Kow Soy* (Cow-Soy), Mom's eyes sparkled with recognition. "Let's see if it tastes like my recipe," she said, her smile full of warmth and nostalgia.

We settled onto plastic stools, bowls steaming in front of us. The rich, fragrant broth cradled minced pork and thick rice noodles, each bite carrying the memory of cold nights back in Colorado when Mom's cooking brought comfort and warmth. But here, the flavor carried something more—a deep, unshakable sense of home.

Later, as the sun slipped below the horizon, we found ourselves by the Mekong River. Dad struck up a conversation with a boatman winding down his day, and soon we were floating slowly on the dark water. The river mirrored the fiery sky, smooth and endless. Homes lined the banks, smoke swirling from chimneys as families prepared their evening meals. The sound was profound, broken only by the gentle hum of the motor.

Yet beneath the river's serene beauty lay a heavy

history. This same water had been a lifeline—and a line of peril—for so many. It was that same river Mom and Dad had crossed long ago, hidden beneath a tarp, guided by a stranger's kindness and courage. As we drifted, I felt the weight of their sacrifices settle over me, a silent testament to the journey that had brought us here. They left behind a world fraught with danger and uncertainty so that I could stand in this moment—floating peacefully on a river that once divided life and death.

The next morning, I woke to the persistent crowing of roosters. Back home in Denver, I'd groan at the sound of garbage trucks rattling past my window, dragging myself reluctantly out of bed. But here, the unfamiliar call of the rooster brought an unexpected smile. I scrambled to the window and pushed open the wooden shutters, drinking in the scene: a neighbor's yard lush with vibrant greenery, a small hen house tucked in the corner, and the sun climbing slowly over rooftops, spilling soft pinks and oranges across the sky. It was a sunrise unlike any I'd ever seen from my bedroom window. Turning to Kaela, I shook her gently awake, my eyes wide with wonder. "Look, Kaela—a real wake-up call!"

Our guesthouse was simple—nothing fancy, but perfectly enough. The bathroom arrangement was comically awkward; the showerhead hung directly over the toilet, forcing us into a careful dance to avoid flooding the whole room. We laughed over our clumsy attempts, embracing the quirks rather than resisting them. Somehow, those little imperfections made it feel more real, more connected to the everyday lives of our relatives back home. Compared to many, we were fortunate, and we didn't forget it.

When we finally reached Grandma's house in Chiang Kham, Thailand, excitement filled the room. The entire family had gathered, waiting with open arms and warm smiles. The table was laid with a feast—steaming bowls of fragrant rich stir frys, Lao stews, and cold bottles of Beer Lao. I smiled to myself at the name—technically it should be 'Lao Beer,' but like the language itself, it came with its own rhythm and character.

My uncle teased me from across the dinner table, as I carried on conversations in Lao with a full American accent. That made me smile too. I'm sure it must've been bizarre, seeing a Lao woman sit at dinner and speak the language with an American accent.

Grandma's house stood proudly painted a gentle blue, two stories tall, though she no longer ventured upstairs. Age had slowed her steps, and cataracts clouded her once-dark eyes, now faded to a soft gray. Yet her mind remained sharp, her voice steady as she engaged in lively conversation, clearly savoring the home my father had helped build with money sent—a home filled with love.

I looked at her kitchen, it had a lot of similarities to the one Mom had back in Colorado. There were burners and pots that lived outside too.

At dinner, Dad's family shared some interesting stories. Particularly, Dad's earliest story as a little boy.

Dad's siblings—two brothers and a sister—had a different father than him. They shared the same mother, yes, but my dad was the odd one out. As a result, I carried within me a thread of Burmese blood, twenty-five percent, from my biological grandfather.

Dad's father was a Burmese politician, a man who left my grandma long before Dad was old enough to hold any memories of him. When he vanished, Grandma never saw him again. It wasn't until years later that Dad discovered he had a half-brother living in Burma, growing up with the father he'd never known—another family, another life, separated by borders, language, and fate.

Of course, Dad rarely spoke of this past. He carries it like a man hauling a heavy bag over his shoulder, never setting it down, never complaining. What I do know is that he loved his stepdad—a steady presence who stayed for many years and raised him with the other children he had with my grandma. He was a man who forged a long and meaningful bond with my grandma and with Dad himself. He treated Dad like he was his own. That love became a foundation, a different kind of family strength and belonging into our story.

Though my Lao was imperfect and my upbringing deeply American, I felt an undeniable sense of belonging in Laos. It was strange—how a place I had never truly lived could feel so familiar, how the hazy air seemed to carry memories I had never lived but somehow recognized. And I knew this feeling wasn't accidental. It was because my parents had carried Laos with them, across oceans and years—not only in the language they spoke or the meals they prepared, but in the way they raised us, in the values they passed down, in the unspoken truth that no matter where we settled, our roots remained tied to this land. Every sound, every scent, every shared meal wove together the fragments of my identity in ways I had never fully understood before.

This journey to Mom and Dad's birthplace carried a weight beyond sightseeing—it was a reckoning. For so long, I wrestled with the challenge of defining myself—caught between an American life and a Lao heritage that sometimes felt distant. But standing on this soil, walking these streets, hearing the familiar voices of family, I finally found the last piece of me. I felt whole. The questions I had carried for years started to settle. Seeing Laos with my own eyes gifted me something I had long needed: perspective.

I witnessed my family's strength—their ability to find joy even when material things were scarce. I saw the revelatory beauty in simplicity, in a way of life that prized community above wealth or status. And for the first time, I felt a fierce, unshakable pride in being Lao-American. It was a pride I needed to claim openly—because being first generation means living a unique journey, one of discovery, adapting, and belonging across two worlds.

I had come to Laos searching—for answers, for a sense of connection, maybe even for a kind of closure I couldn't quite name. But what I found was something deeper: a part of myself I didn't know had been missing.

I didn't leave with all the answers in the world, but I left with something better—an extension of home.

Saying goodbye was harder than I imagined. As the plane lifted into the sky and the outline of Laos faded beneath the clouds, I felt a pull in my chest—an ache, like I was leaving behind a place I had just started to know. But I also carried something with me. Not souvenirs or snapshots, but something lasting: a rooted, undeniable understanding of where I came from and the people I come from.

And in the end, that was more than I ever expected to find.

8 | The Aftermath

Today, even the land itself carries painful memories of the past. Beneath the soil of Laos lie remnants of a war that was never officially declared, and yet left a brutal, lasting imprint. During the Secret War, more than two million tons of bombs were dropped across the country. The ground still contains hidden landmines, nearly 30% of which never detonated. They remain unseen, rusting beneath fields and jungles, tucked into the ground like landlocked killers—silent, patient, and deadly.

For decades after, a single wrong step could mean the difference between life and death. Children picking fruit, farmers tilling their land, families trying to build futures on top of shattered ground—so many have been injured or killed by these invisible landmines. So today, the legacy still endures.

Though clearance efforts have made progress, nearly 50 lives are still lost every year. This is an improvement from the 310 lives lost in 2008—but still, every statistic is a person. A story interrupted. Nearly 40% of the victims are children—too young to understand the danger, too innocent to see the war still lingering beneath their feet.

This is not a distant history—it's my family's history. It's our inheritance. My classmates didn't know where Laos was, let alone what had happened there. I spent nineteen years of my life in the American education system, from Kindergarten through my Master's degree. Throughout that entire time, I never once saw Laos mentioned in any of the textbooks.

The Secret War that changed the course of my parents' lives was buried—not only beneath the earth, but in the void of American memory. Laos was treated as a footnote, if it were mentioned at all. A tiny, faraway place that became a pawn in a much larger geopolitical game. But to us, it was everything. It was home, it was loss, it was survival—all in one.

I recognize the burden of erasure. That absence isn't just about invisibility—it's about the ways generational pain festers when it goes unnamed. The shame I carried growing up, the confusion I felt about where I was supposed to be, the worry of not being fluent in my parents' language—it all stemmed, in part, from a history that had been systematically ignored.

But there is a glimmer of hope. In recent years, a big step toward recognition was taken. Legislation was passed requiring Lao history to be taught in schools. For the first time, our story—our trauma and our strength—will be shared in classrooms, taking part in the larger American narrative where it has always belonged. This shift means that the Secret War won't just be passed down through secret family stories or fading photos. It will be studied, acknowledged, remembered.

For so many of us, this wasn't just a curriculum change. It was validation. It was healing. It meant we were no longer invisible stories. I look forward to the children who come along after us—the Lao, the Hmong, and all refugee-born children trying to make sense of who they are.

I think of them opening a textbook and seeing their grandparents' history honored. I think of a classroom where no one has to shrink when asked, "Where are you from?" or struggle to explain a war their teachers never learned about. That vision makes me optimistic. Elated, even. More than just about remembering the past—but about shaping the future and preserving our story. And for the first time in a long time, it seems possible.

The war in Laos was never truly about saving Lao lives. It didn't fulfill its intent for justice, protection, or liberation. Instead it was about fulfilling a strategy to halt the spread of communism and disrupting Vietnamese communist supply lines. Laos became the battleground for someone else's war. A proxy war. A secret one that cost families dearly.

By the time it ended, Laos held a grim title: the most heavily bombed country per capita in human history. Entire villages wiped off the map. And the lessons of that war were buried beneath layers of classified CIA documents, veterans' unspoken trauma, and the world's collective indifference. But that did not erase the truth. It only delayed its reckoning.

When Laos fell to communism in 1975, it fell with Cambodia. Still, the infamous Domino Theory, which had once been used to justify U.S. involvement in Laos, ultimately proved flawed. Communism did not sweep across all of Southeast Asia as predicted—it never claimed Thailand, Malaysia, or Indonesia. But the human cost was real. The true casualties were not governments or ideologies—they were the people and their families. Those who fled with nothing but the clothes on their backs. and those who were separated from family members who either died or refused to flee at all.

Among the many who sought refuge in America, the Lao and Hmong were some of the most vulnerable along with many others. All of them with no grasp of the English language. They arrived with no money and no formal education—as many had been just children when the bombs fell. They had no résumés to offer, only hands hardened by labor and hearts broken by war. They came carrying trauma so deep and raw, it had no words in either language. Yet they came anyway, seeking asylum for safety in a land that did not always understand them.

Incidentally, survival in America meant starting from absolute zero. Navigating an entirely foreign culture, decoding the systems of healthcare, education, and employment—all while carrying their invisible scars. PTSD ran deep but unspoken. There were no Lao-speaking therapists, no community mental health programs tailored to Southeast Asian trauma. Pain was something to swallow, not speak.

Yet still, they endured. Their faith—and often their only real support—came from strangers. Faith-based organizations like the U.S. Conference of Catholic

Bishops, Lutheran Immigration and Refugee Service, and Church World Service stepped in to fill the void, offering more than just housing and job referrals. They offered kindness. Humanity. A lifeline. Families like mine were lucky to be matched with sponsors who cared. That generosity gave us the tools to rebuild—not only our lives, but our sense of belonging in a country that wasn't made with us in mind.

When Dad and I visited the Colorado State Capitol, there was a room in the heart of the building, where photos of each U.S. president were hung up. The framed photos were proudly displayed in rows on the wall. I stood closer towards the end, looking at the photo of President Obama. Dad walked a few feet ahead of me, scanning each one. "Who are you looking for Dad?" I reached to see if I could help. "I want to find Gerald Ford and Jimmy Carter." he said.

It dawned on me, he was looking for the Presidents who were in office when he, Saeng, and Mom arrived. It was Gerald Ford who was president when the first Lao immigrants were welcome to arrive in the U.S. and it was Jimmy Carter who continued to oversee refugee settlement efforts.

The Secret War may have nearly erased us, but we are still here. And we carry our stories forward, not as victims, but as witnesses and survivors.

For those who came, America was a lifeline—an open door, yes, but also an uphill climb. It asked everything of them: their language, their labor, their ability to endure. And yet, they answered with quiet determination. For those who stayed behind, Laos remained a land of resilience—scarred by war, slowed by poverty, but still standing. Still singing. Still surviving.

For those like me, who were born here, they landed in a space between those worlds. The child of survivors, growing up surrounded by the invisible ghost of a war we never asked to be a part of—but somehow still carried. The trauma passed down in every gesture made with their head hanging down, in the way our parents double-checked door locks, or panicked if we ever spoke negatively about politics. We inherited stories that were rarely told, and when they were, they came out in pieces—half-shared, choked by memory.

I spent so much time trying to piece those stories together, trying to understand who we were, in a country that never seemed to know what we were.

There were no chapters about us in school books, no faces like ours on television. It was as if we came from nowhere and everywhere at once—a foot in two cultures, but a home in neither.

But on my return to Laos, through raising my daughter, through writing these pages—I've come to understand that our past is not just something to carry as a burden. It is something to hold. To honor. To speak aloud.

Because in those silent fields where bombs still lie buried, in the laughter of aunties cooking over open fires, in the tears of my parents returning to a church in Seattle three decades later—there is power. There is beauty. There is history that refuses to die.

I do not come from silence. I come from strength. The legacy I carry is not just one of displacement, but of perseverance. It is the story of people who refused to disappear. Who rebuilt lives from ashes and taught their children to dream in two languages. Who stitched identity out of fragments and offered up their joy as an act of rebellion. That story lives in me—and now, in these pages.

This is why I tell it. Not because our story is finished, but because it is finally being heard.

For my parents.
For my daughter.
For the Lao community that continues to rise.
And for every child who ever wondered if their story mattered.

It does. And it always will.

Acknowledgements

A heartfelt thank you for taking the time to read this book. I'm truly grateful for your interest in our story and for your patience as I've navigated through my emotions and thoughts along the way.

To my family—Mom, Dad, Kaela, Saeng, and Jay—thank you for being the unwavering motivation and strength in my life. And to my small but mighty support system, your presence has been invaluable on this journey.

www.ingramcontent.com/pod-product-compliance
Lightning Source LLC
Chambersburg PA
CBHW020242010526
44107CB00039B/1465/J